MW00874066

# MINDFUL PARENTING FOR ADHD CHILDREN

## A PROVEN GUIDE WITH DIALECTICAL BEHAVIORAL THERAPY SKILLS AND MINDFULNESS ACTIVITIES TO MANAGE AND IMPROVE EMOTIONAL REGULATION, FOCUS, AND SELF-CONTROL FOR KIDS

CATHERINE L. ABBOTT

© **Copyright 2022 - All rights reserved.**

The content contained within this book may not be reproduced, duplicated, or transmitted without direct written permission from the author or the publisher.

Under no circumstances will any blame or legal responsibility be held against the publisher, or author, for any damages, reparation, or monetary loss due to the information contained within this book, either directly or indirectly.

## Special Credit – Book cover:

The cover of this book has been designed using assets from Freepik.com – A big thank you to them for providing this beautiful art

## Legal Notice:

This book is copyright protected. It is only for personal use. You cannot amend, distribute, sell, use, quote, or paraphrase any part, or the content within this book, without the author or publisher's permission.

## Disclaimer Notice:

Please note that the information contained within this document is for educational and entertainment purposes only. All effort has been executed to present accurate, up-to-date, reliable, complete information. No warranties of any kind are declared or implied. Readers acknowledge that the author is not rendering legal, financial, medical, or professional advice. The content within this book has been derived from various sources. Please consult a licensed professional before attempting any techniques outlined in this book.

By reading this document, the reader agrees that under no circumstances is the author responsible for any losses, direct or indirect, that are incurred due to the use of the information in this document, including, but not limited to, errors, omissions, or inaccuracies.

# CONTENTS

# Your Free Gift Bundle

Thank you so much for your purchase. The fact that you are taking time out of your busy life to read my book means the world to me.

Knowing how precious your time is and as a way of saying thanks for your purchase, I'm offering my **Ultimate Family Morning Routine** AND my **Ultimate Family Night Routine** for FREE to my readers.

To get instant access just go to:

**https://mindfulparentingbooks.com/free-gift**

**I hope these free guides will help you find great ideas that you and your family can implement to better your lives.**

# INTRODUCTION

It's the start of arguably the most dreaded time of the year for many parents: your child is writing exams at school. You are already exhausted from screaming, begging, and pleading with your child to concentrate on their studies, and the exams have only just begun. *How will we make it through the next week?* You ask yourself over and over.

You listen to your friends or colleagues talking about this dreaded time and how they are following specific study schedules. "We are hoping for another top-of-the-class position," one explains. Secretly, all you are hoping for is that your child will pass their grade. This frustrates you, as you know very well that your child is extremely intelligent. Your child understands their work well when they sit still and concentrate. But this rarely happens...

Since your child has been diagnosed with attention deficit hyperactivity disorder (ADHD), you've tried many methods to help them cope with life more successfully. Unfortunately, most of these methods have been without much improvement or success. You still end up yelling at your child as they spend hours focusing on ants walking on the ground instead of their important schoolwork.

"Today is going to be different. Today will be good," you almost chant to yourself on your way to pick up your child from school. However, less than an hour later, it's back to your daily routine of begging and fighting over their lack of concentration, their joking attitude toward their work, their hyperactivity, and their time blindness. "How can it take you an hour to write three words?" You ask your child. "Please concentrate!"

Eventually, after more time wasted without any proper studying, your frustration gets the better of you, and you shout, "I can't do this anymore!" What raises your blood pressure even more is how your child goes from being seemingly unfazed by your now extreme exasperation to reacting with explosive violence within minutes. "Something has to change," you tell yourself as you are yet again thinking of ideas on how to help your child.

If this sounds anything like your life, you've come to the right place. You can transform your and your child's lives by learning simple, practical, and simplistic ways of parenting your child with ADHD. This detailed guide will give you step-by-step instructions on how to create and maintain self-control and raise happy, thriving children despite the challenges that their neurodiversity may bring. Even if you are only starting out on your journey to mindful parenting, the tips and strategies discussed in this book will be life-changing.

I've been in the exact same position you are in. My son was given a diagnosis of autism spectrum disorder (ASD) and ADHD 17 years ago. This diagnosis left me confused and scampering around in a state of panic. I felt overwhelmed and powerless, much like many other parents in the same situation.

I was determined to provide my child with the right type of care. I was motivated and set out on a quest to learn everything I could about both conditions. Surrounded by an understanding and loving family, my son had a wonderful childhood and coped well among his peers.

Spurred by this success, I've made it my life's mission to help families going through the same situation. I'm passionate about helping parents and children surmount the challenges of ASD, ADHD, and other mental health conditions such as depression, anxiety, anger, worry, and fear. I'm an advocate of mindful, interactive parenting and treatment options such as dialectical behavioral therapy (DBT).

I started helping others by speaking at community events, writing blogs, and eventually publishing my first book in 2020. These are all based on my extensive research, personal experiences, and the success stories I've been fortunate to be part of.

My life motto is that to be able to help their child, parents need the right knowledge and support. It's up to parents who have successfully gone through that phase to help them. Now, I want to help you overcome the challenges that your child's ADHD may bring.

In this book, I've divided the information into three parts to ensure it is easy to understand and reference:

- **A complete overview of ADHD,** including common mistakes many parents make after receiving the diagnosis, as well as overlapping conditions that you should be aware of.
- **Tips on how you can help your child thrive**, including how you can help your child to live their lives in a socially acceptable manner and practice helpful mindful skills and techniques taught during dialectical behavioral therapy.
- How to help your child to **manage their sometimes explosive behavior,** as well as tips on how they can improve their emotional regulation and self-control.

Parenting in general can be a difficult and stressful experience. This can be even more so if you have a child with neurodiversity. Luckily, it doesn't have to be that way. The first step in raising a thriving child and preventing explosive behavior is fully comprehending what ADHD is, as well as its symptoms and possible causes. If you are ready to reach your parenting goals and change your current outputs, let's get straight into it.

# 1

# ACCEPTING AND UNDERSTANDING THE DIAGNOSIS

You may have heard the term "ADHD" used often without giving it too much thought. This changes immediately after one of your loved ones, such as your child, gets this diagnosis. You may have thought your child was slightly different from their peers and may even have noticed that they struggle a bit more with schoolwork, but you never thought neurodiversity would ever be diagnosed in your child.

Many different reasons may lead you to the doctor's office for an evaluation. Your child's teacher may have suggested you have them checked out, or you may also have noticed during homework that your child struggles to sit still. Your child's explosive behavior and impulsivity may also have led you to wonder if something is wrong. The global COVID-19 pandemic has also resulted in many parents reaching out for help, as homeschooling during this time may have changed the way you view your child's behavior in a completely different way.

Whatever convinces you to take your child for a checkup, the results remain the same: Hearing that your child has been diagnosed with ADHD can send shockwaves through your body. Suddenly, you may be overcome with fears for your child's future, how you will go about parenting your little human, and how your child will be able to adjust to social norms.

Due to all the potential unknown factors that can come with such a diagnosis and the different treatment options available, it's important that you remain calm. Take it step-by-step, and before you jump to complicated strategies to implement in your daily routine, make sure you take your time to understand this disorder completely. Knowing exactly what to expect can not only help you adjust your parenting style accordingly and introduce new techniques, but also allow you to celebrate the positive attributes that people with ADHD have. Over time, your child may even be able to use their symptoms, such as hyperfocus, to their advantage.

## IS ADHD A SERIOUS CONDITION?

ADHD is a very common neurodevelopmental disorder that most commonly affects children but can only be diagnosed in adulthood. It is a chronic condition, meaning it will last for years and can even be present for the rest of the child's life.

Even though it isn't a rare condition, the Center for Disease Control in the United States regards it as a serious mental health condition (CDC, 2019). This is largely due to the increased risk of injury. Research found that children with ADHD are 30% more likely to sustain injuries than children without this neurodiversity (*Is ADHD a serious condition?*, 2016).

Despite ADHD being a neurodiversity condition in that it affects brain functionality, it is officially classified as a mental health illness. Mental health illnesses are defined as treatable health conditions that impact your behavior, emotions, and/or thought processes, which can have a severe impact on your quality of life and your ability to deal with stressful situations and maintain relationships. Many people prefer to refer to ADHD as a disorder instead of an illness due to the stigma that is often associated with the latter word.

To clinically diagnose ADHD, healthcare professionals use the Diagnostic and Statistical Manual of Mental

Disorders (DSM-5). The medical specialists usually involved in making this diagnosis include your general practitioner, pediatrician, psychiatrist, psychologist, and occupational therapist. Generally, patients under the age of 16 must have six or more of the symptoms listed on the DSM-5, while the criteria for patients older than 17 would be five symptoms. These symptoms must be present for at least six months and be present in more than one aspect of their lives before a diagnosis should be made.

The DSM-5 criteria for ADHD include (Herndon, 2021)

- inability to pay attention
- make careless mistakes
- lack of attention to detail
- struggle to follow instructions
- difficulty with organizational tasks
- avoidance of specific tasks, particularly those requiring attention for long periods of time
- often loses items
- easily distracted
- extreme forgetfulness
- fidgets or inability to sit still
- standing up or moving around when they're supposed to stay seated
- restlessness
- excessive talking

- can't play or keep quiet while taking part in activities
- blurts answers before a question is asked
- interrupts others while they're talking
- can't wait their turn

## WHY HAS THIS TERM BECOME SO LOOSELY USED

Even though ADHD is considered a serious condition, the term is used flippantly by many people who don't actually have this mental disease. Neurotypical people will often say things like, "I'm so ADHD right now" or "I'm having an ADHD moment." This can be very disheartening to those who have ADHD or have a loved one with the condition, as it may feel like others are either not understanding the severity of the symptoms or simply don't care. This can take a big toll on the person with ADHD's self-esteem.

Due to the lack of understanding of the disorder, many people don't feel comfortable speaking about their condition. This is often due to the misconception that people with ADHD are lazy, should simply try harder, or should pull themselves together. These misconceptions result in neurotypical people often claiming to "act ADHD" when they aren't finishing their tasks. What they often don't understand is that ADHD is much more than simply not finishing tasks or forgetting your lunch at home. And every time they stereotype this condition by calming down to have an "ADHD moment," they are minimizing the actual effect that this disorder has on those with this neurodiversity. This stereotype completely disregards all the anxiety, social difficulties, and often lack of coping mechanisms that generally come with ADHD.

The misconceptions around ADHD, as well as the stereotype many neurotypical people place on it, make it even more important to fully understand the different subtypes of this disorder and the extent of the symptoms your child may have.

## THE THREE SUBTYPES

You may have been surprised when your child received their ADHD diagnosis, as they don't seem overly hyperactive. However, not all children (or people in general) with ADHD struggle with fidgeting and sitting still. Let's look at the three different subtypes of this condition:

- **Predominantly inattentive and distractible**: This is when your child will struggle with organizing, finishing a task, concentrating, and following instructions. This child will easily forget things, including belongings, tasks, and commands. They won't be unusually hyperactive or impulsive.

- **Predominantly hyperactive-impulsive**: If your child has this subtype, they will likely fidget a lot and struggle to sit still. Your younger child may constantly be running, climbing, or jumping, while your older child may struggle to sit still at school or while doing homework. They may constantly feel restless and struggle to control their impulses. They will interrupt conversations and have difficulty waiting their turn. These children will be more prone to accidents and injuries. They don't struggle with distractibility or inattention.
- **Combined ADHD**: If your child has combined ADHD, both of the other types of ADHD will be equally present in their lives. This is the most common subtype of ADHD.

## ADHD AND THE BRAIN

As I've mentioned, ADHD is a neurodevelopmental disorder in that it affects the way the brain works and the production of neurotransmitters such as dopamine. Dopamine plays a major role in the brain's reward and pleasure centers. The dysregulation of or lack of dopamine then results in inattention, difficulty controlling emotions, impulsivity, and hyperactivity.

Apart from the imbalance in neurotransmitters such as dopamine, the physical structure of the brain of a person with ADHD may also be different. Certain areas of the brain may be smaller or take longer to develop.

## DOES MY KID HAVE ADHD?

Understanding the typical behavior that a child with ADHD may show can help you identify issues of concern within your child. It can be helpful to keep a thorough record of your child's behavioral problems and to discuss this with your child's teacher, as this will help your doctor in their clinical evaluation of your child and make a possible diagnosis.

The signs you should look out for in your child will largely depend on their age. Also, keep in mind that just because your child may be displaying some of the signs of ADHD, that doesn't necessarily mean that they do have the condition. Your healthcare professional will look at many different factors and may send your child for hearing and eye tests before confirming any suspicions you may have.

When dealing with young children—especially those under the age of four—it can be difficult to determine whether they are behaving in a manner that is typical for the developmental stage they may be in or whether their behavior does signal a bigger problem. A general rule of thumb that many pediatricians and occupational therapists apply to these young children is to look at their safety.

If their seemingly over-the-top behavior puts them in greater danger of injury, you may want to look at tests. All children fall and get bumps and scrapes as they learn what their bodies are capable of and as their muscles and coordination develop, but frequently breaking bones or getting more serious cuts can put your child's health at risk.

If your child shows extreme aggression towards friends in the same age group, is overly friendly or trusting of strangers, or can't hop on one leg by the time they are four, they may show signs of atypical development that may warrant going for tests.

Other behavioral signs you can look out for in your young child or toddler can include

- being easily distracted.
- lack of focus on activities.
- inability to sit still.
- difficulty following simple instructions.
- constant fidgeting with their hands.
- moving their feet a lot.

- being unacceptably loud in circumstances that would require them to talk softly.
- excessive talking.
- inability to wait for and take turns.
- interrupting conversations.

As the child gets older, the signs of ADHD can change. This can be due to your child's learning how to cope with their former behavioral problems easier and their increased brain development. It can, however, also happen that your child's ADHD may get worse as they get older. As a result, they may only get diagnosed as an adolescent, teenager, or even an adult.

Signs that you should take note of in your older child can include

- inattention when busy with schoolwork.
- making mistakes frequently.
- difficulty completing tasks.
- trouble with managing time effectively.
- organizational problems.
- often forgetting things.
- losing possessions frequently.
- emotional sensitivity and dysregulation.
- difficulty in social situations.
- increased frustration.

- appearing to be immature when compared to their friends.
- not listening attentively.

One of the biggest signs of ADHD in older children is lack of concentration and struggling with their academic performance. However, this can also be difficult to truly measure, as you may feel unsure of your child's ability and IQ. A general rule to use here is to look at how your child performs or remembers things they are interested in. If they can recite the lyrics to their favorite songs and repeat lines from a movie they enjoy, but can't seem to learn their oral or study for tests, it can be time to take them for an evaluation.

## ADHD SYMPTOMS BY AGE

Once your child has been diagnosed with ADHD, it's important to know what symptoms you may expect in the different age groups so that you can not only be aware of what to expect but also fully prepare for it.

- **Toddlers and Preschoolers**: Doctors will often avoid making a diagnosis while the child is so young. As I've mentioned, your child may seem exceptionally busy and seems to always be on the go. They may be so restless that they won't even be able to sit still for a bedtime story that they aren't interested in. However, if they are really interested in a game, story, or toy, they may be able to sit still for extended periods of time.

- **Elementary School Kids**: Most children are diagnosed when they are in elementary school. This is when they are required to sit still at school and concentrate on their schoolwork. ADHD with extreme hyperactivity will likely be diagnosed a lot earlier than the subtype with inattention, as an overly active child may disrupt the classroom, resulting in the teacher having to take action a lot sooner. As the schoolwork gets more difficult, a child with inattention and concentration difficulties will struggle more to cope, get more frustrated, and make more mistakes. For example, they may know exactly how to solve a math problem and understand what equation to use, but will then make "silly mistakes" by using the wrong numbers in a word sum or multiplying instead of dividing. They may also get a lot more emotional and confrontational, which can lead to problems with their friends and at home.

- **Teenagers**: Hyperactivity often gets better as the child gets older, but they may still be more restless than their peers. Problems with time management, organization, and concentration can become more severe in this age group, as their schoolwork will not only get more, but it will also get more difficult. However, they may have no issues with completing tasks that offer them immediate results or that they are very interested in. In general, teenagers tend to struggle with emotional regulation. This can be even more so for teenagers with ADHD, which can result in a lot of frustration for the child and parents and cause conflict at home. Due to their impulsivity, they may also engage in more risky behavior, including using substances, stealing, and having unsafe sex.

## ADHD IN GIRLS VS. BOYS

Your child's gender can have a big impact on how the symptoms present and their diagnosis. According to the Centers for Disease Control and Prevention in the United States, boys are up to three times more likely to be diagnosed with ADHD than girls (Kinman, 2012). This isn't due to boys being more susceptible to the condition, but rather that the symptoms in girls are often viewed as more subtle and, therefore, not as easily identified and not diagnosed as often. Let's compare how the condition typically manifests in girls and boys.

## BOYS WITH ADHD: GIRLS WITH ADHD

| Boys With ADHD | Girls With ADHD |
|---|---|
| Externalized symptoms, such as running and being impulsive | Internalized symptoms, such as inattentiveness and low self-esteem |
| More physically aggressive | More verbally aggressive |
| Tend to air their frustrations more | Tend to keep their frustrations bottled up |
| Symptoms are often missed due to the stereotype of boys being more energetic | Symptoms are often missed due to them simply seeming "spaced out" |
| Some boys lack the hyperactivity but show severe inattention | Some girls present with symptoms related to hyperactivity |

Please note that the symptoms discussed above are a generalized view of the condition and how it manifests differently among genders. It may be completely different for your child.

## UNDERSTANDING THE ROOT CAUSES AND RISK FACTORS

There are many different causes and risk factors for ADHD, and although many research projects on the matter are still ongoing, many have concluded that genetics play the biggest role. If either—especially when both—of the parents have ADHD, the child will have a much bigger risk of also having ADHD. What makes this more difficult for families to cope with is when the parent has never officially been diagnosed with this condition and therefore not only struggles with aspects of their own life but also may not know how they can help their child.

Problems during pregnancy can also increase the risk of the child having ADHD. This can include when the pregnant mother consumes alcohol, uses tobacco, uses drugs, or is exposed to lead. A child that is born prematurely or has a low birth weight can have a bigger risk of being diagnosed with the condition. Brain injury can also increase this risk.

Although many people believe that consuming too much sugar, having too much screen time, or living in poverty can increase the chances of ADHD, research done on the topic doesn't confirm this. These factors can, however, increase the severity of the symptoms or result in the child not getting the proper treatment they need to cope with the condition.

## ACCEPTING THE DIAGNOSIS

Once your child is diagnosed with ADHD, it is important to accept the diagnosis. This way, you will be able to focus on how you can help your child improve the quality of their life and their schoolwork instead of fighting the diagnosis and not getting your child the treatment they may need. You will likely see a drastic improvement within days of starting their treatment.

Let's look at four things you should make a conscious effort to accept immediately:

- **Your child's brain chemistry and structure are different from those of neurotypical people.** This doesn't mean there is anything wrong with them. They aren't broken. They are simply wired differently.
- **Your child's ADHD doesn't define who they are.** It is just one aspect of their life. Yes, this one aspect can have a big impact on their life, but there are many other things that make up their identity.
- **Your child's ADHD may result in more ups and downs,** as you will likely both struggle to navigate the different symptoms and find ways to decrease the impact their symptoms will have on their lives.
- **ADHD doesn't have to be viewed negatively.** If you can help your child, they can learn to use many of their symptoms to their advantage. Their hyperfocus can help them solve problems; their time blindness can make them determined to keep at a task until it's complete, their high-energy levels can help them to reach unbelievable goals, and their impulsivity can help them take the right risks to achieve phenomenal success.

You can help your child to find the silver lining
that their ADHD will bring.

Even though it is important that you accept your child's
diagnosis, it is important to remain realistic. Acceptance
won't remove the stress that can come with such a diagnosis. It can, however, make a difference in how you react
and parent your child.

Accepting the diagnosis can also help you celebrate the
small milestones and regain your sense of humor. If your
child remembers to pack their school bag correctly, make a
big deal about it. It's a much bigger accomplishment than
you realize. The more you celebrate your child's small
milestones, the more their confidence will improve. They
will be more motivated to take on bigger tasks if their self-
esteem gets boosted regularly.

2

# MISTAKES TO AVOID AFTER THE DIAGNOSIS

Hearing that your child has a potentially lifelong mental health condition such as ADHD can set off a rollercoaster of emotions within you. On the one hand, you may actually feel relieved, as you've finally found the reason for your child's behavior and struggles, while on the other hand, you may fear the unknown of this condition. While still on this rollercoaster, you need to pull yourself together for the sake of your child and protect their mental health at all times.

Unfortunately, as much as you may mean well, you are likely to make mistakes on your journey toward helping your child. Many of these mistakes are often made when parents have to explain ADHD to their child. To help you through this, we will now explore how ADHD can affect a child's mental health, the five most common mistakes many parents make, and give you tips on how you can explain this disorder to your child.

## EFFECTS OF ADHD ON A CHILD'S MENTAL HEALTH

Let's first look at the impact ADHD can have on a child's mental health. This is important to understand, as you may unintentionally and unknowingly affect your child's mental wellness in the way you parent them and the mistakes you may make.

A recent study on the effects of ADHD on mental well-being showed that 80% of children with ADHD will be diagnosed with another psychiatric condition at some point during their lives (ADDitude, n.d.). Some of the mental, behavioral, and emotional concerns that these children may have or develop include

- behavioral disorder, which can lead to delinquent behavior
- mood disorders, such as anxiety and depression
- being bullied by their peers
- increased risk of substance abuse as they grow older
- risky sexual behavior
- suicide and self-harm

Since these conditions most often start to develop during adolescence, it is important to work on improving your child's mental well-being from an early age. This way, you can lay the important groundwork that will either reduce the severity of any mental health illnesses they may develop later on or give you the foundation of a strong and healthy relationship with your child so that you will be better equipped to help them through these struggles.

## MISTAKES MANY PARENTS MAKE AFTER DIAGNOSIS

A good start to looking after your child's mental health is to try your best to avoid the common mistakes many parents of children with ADHD often make. Even though the mistakes you may make might be very specific to your situation, reading through the five most common mistakes many parents make can help you identify things that you are doing wrong and how you can work on avoiding those mistakes.

### *Losing Your Temper*

It is natural to get angry when your child's hyperactivity takes over, especially in situations where they are required to sit still, when their impulsivity puts them in physical harm, or when they are supposed to concentrate on their schoolwork, but continuously talks about unrelated topics or stare out the window for hours without getting any work done.

Children with ADHD's temporal lobes take longer to mature and may only reach maturity at the age of 25. This part of the brain forms the center where memories are stored, emotions are regulated, and auditory processing takes place. As a result, these children will need extra assistance with these types of tasks.

Since your mature brain has the capacity to regulate your emotions, you should work at managing your feelings whenever you feel yourself getting upset with your child. Try to be as calm as possible before you address the problem with your child. Stop what you are busy with and practice some deep breathing techniques to calm yourself down before you react. If you need to, remove yourself from the situation for a few minutes to regroup.

Once you've calmed down, help your child to do the same. Help them by teaching them deep breathing techniques. After they've calmed down, discuss what happened, what made them so upset, why their reaction was wrong, and guide them in finding better ways to react going forward.

### *Misunderstanding Their Problems*

When you get frustrated with your child for not concentrating on their work, being impulsive or hyperactive, or being overly forgetful, try your best to remember that they aren't behaving in this way on purpose. When your child thinks about the holiday you will have in two months' time when they are supposed to concentrate on their homework, their wandering mind is caused by their inability to focus on their work, not because they're too lazy to work. When they forget their school project at home, they aren't lazy. The slow development of their frontal lobes makes it difficult for them to remember things.

To help them, you should always remind yourself of the problems they may have that aren't within their control. To make this easier for you, think about the problems in your life that you have little to no control over. Do you give yourself some slack on these things? This should be the same for your child. If you can accept who you are and that there are things in your life you can't help, you should work at accepting your child and the things they can't control.

If you don't have ADHD or any other form of neurodiversity, it can be difficult to understand your child's inability to sit still or to concentrate. However, if you constantly remind yourself of the symptoms of ADHD that your child has, you can become more accepting of them and their struggles. Your child isn't being difficult on purpose, and their struggles will likely cause as much frustration for you as for them. Accept the fact that your child may take longer to develop specific skills, and help them where necessary with this.

### *Excluding Their Ideas and Suggestions*

Your child may deal with severe feelings of inadequacy and even inferiority in many aspects of their life, such as academic work, social interactions, and emotional regulation. They may constantly feel—or even hear—that they've missed the mark or that their attempts aren't good enough.

You may mean well to be telling them how they should do things and what you think will help them, but if you don't have ADHD yourself or have an exceptionally deep understanding of how their brains work, your ideas and suggestions may not work for them at all. By doing this, you may even cause more damage than good, as they may feel even more inadequate when your ideas don't make a difference and decrease their symptoms.

Talk to your child about what they are experiencing and ask them if they have suggestions as to how they can decrease the severity of their symptoms. They may surprise you with ideas of what may work for them. Always remember that you aren't living their realities with them and, as a result, won't truly understand what they think may help them. Even if you believe their ideas are unlikely to produce results, consider giving them a chance. Work with them and discuss their suggestions. If they see their opinions are listened to, it will give them more buy-in to sort the problem out.

Working with them gives you the opportunity to change the problem and solution from "you" to "we." It will no longer be a case of imposing your ideas by saying, "You need to do this." Instead, it will allow you to use sentences such as, "We can give this a try." Remember, as the parent, you will have the final say in what should happen, but by showing your child that you value their input, they may cooperate more.

### *Not Being Consistent*

In general, children with ADHD thrive on the predictability of set routines and rules. The same goes for disciplining their child. If you are not consistent in how you discipline your child and what rules they should follow, you may find them pushing boundaries and acting out even more. They may pester you to the point where they think you'll give in or not take you seriously when you threaten them with specific punishment when they are misbehaving.

Be as consistent as you possibly can, but never aim for perfection. There is no such thing as a perfect parent. There will be times when you will give in or allow things you wouldn't normally do. As long as you try your best to be as consistent as possible most of the time, you are doing a good job. Never threaten your child with consequences that you can't or won't enforce. Be realistic in any punishments. Always remember that they are already having difficulty learning and understanding their world; don't make this trial-and-error learning even more difficult by being inconsistent.

### *Focusing Only on the Outcome*

Many parents are overly focused on the outcomes. These can be outcomes achieved in your child's academics or outcomes of treatments for their ADHD. It is always important to remember that the optimal treatment for ADHD can vary from child to child, so starting out with treatment can be very much a case of trial-and-error. Never get disheartened when your first treatment option is unsuccessful or when it takes longer to achieve the desired results.

Instead, focus on the small changes and improvements there might be. If you hover too much over the final result, your child may get demotivated or lose momentum. But if you set small goals along the way and celebrate the small wins, your child will likely want to show more improvements and work harder on reducing the impact of their symptoms.

If your child remembers their school project, you can simply say you are proud of them. If they remember to bring their dishes to the kitchen or put their dirty clothes in the laundry hamper, you can acknowledge this by saying *thanks* or how you're so happy you don't have to fight about it that day. By doing this, you are sending two important messages to your child, showing that you're aware of their efforts and that you're happy and proud of them.

## EXPLAINING ADHD TO YOUR CHILD

It is important to discuss your child's condition with them and explain to them what ADHD is in as much detail as their developmental phase requires. For a young child, it may be enough to simply say they may have a bit more energy than their friends, talk a bit more, or struggle a bit more to complete a task. An older child may want more details as to how their brains function differently from their friends, why this is the case, and why they may have this condition for the rest of their lives.

No matter how much detail you decide to give your child, make sure that you never make them feel bad or hopeless about having this condition. Always assure them that what they're experiencing is okay and that you, together with their teachers and doctors, are there to help them.

Always remember that your child doesn't have a medical condition. Avoid telling them, "You have ADHD." Your child simply has ADHD. This condition doesn't define their entire being and shouldn't limit their dreams of what they want to be when they are grown up. Help them to understand that with the correct treatment and help, the severity of their symptoms can be greatly reduced.

Unless your child is older and very mature, avoid using the word "disorder." This word can sound extremely scary for a child, especially when they are still learning about the disorder and what it entails. Instead, you can explain their condition to them by saying that their brains work slightly differently from others' but that this means there are many things they can do that others can't. Bring in some of the positives about having ADHD.

Don't tell your child that they will need medication to be able to learn or behave better. This can make the child seem like something is seriously wrong with them, as they won't be able to live without it. Instead, you can explain to your child that they may have to drink medicine that can make life a bit easier or help them concentrate better. Always remind them that you are working together on reducing their symptoms.

Never let them feel abnormal in any way. In fact, try to avoid using the word "normal" as much as possible in your home. Instead, you can tell them that what they're feeling or how they're behaving is very typical for someone with ADHD.

Always try to focus on the positive aspects that their symptoms may bring. For example, you can tell them that having ADHD can help them come up with many exciting ideas, but that many of them will come at the same time. Tell them that they may struggle a bit more than their friends to decide which of these ideas they should focus on, but that once they are able to learn this skill, they will achieve amazing results and success.

Don't allow your child to use their ADHD as an excuse not to behave properly. Let them know that just because they have the condition, doesn't mean they can do as they please. They will still have to try their best to behave in a manner that is socially acceptable, even if they may struggle more to control their behavior. Remind them that you are there for them and will work with them to find solutions to the problems that land them in trouble.

3

# OVERLAPPING CONDITIONS

Looking after your child's mental wellness is very important, particularly more so when they have a condition such as ADHD. This puts them at a higher risk for suffering comorbid psychiatric conditions, which can include severe disorders such as depression, anxiety, tic disorders, sensory processing disorders, and conduct disorders.

As much as it's important to understand ADHD and how you should always be on the lookout for any signs that their mental wellness is suffering, it is also vital to know and understand what other conditions are often present in children with ADHD. Even though your child's doctor will discuss any comorbidities that they may see evidence of in your child with you, being aware of these conditions and how they may present in your child can help you reach out as soon as you see these signs in your child. To help you with this, we will now look at some of the common overlapping conditions your child with ADHD may have.

## ADHD AND LOW SELF-ESTEEM

Due to many people not fully understanding ADHD, they might blame your child for their symptoms, say things like they should just try to work harder, or that if they simply apply enough willpower, they can overcome their symptoms. This can do severe damage to your child's self-esteem, making it even more difficult for them to cope. Always remember that, just as they didn't choose to have ADHD, they can't simply apply willpower to overcome their struggles. Their brains develop differently, and no amount of willpower or "trying harder" can fix this.

If your child suffers from low self-esteem, they may have even more difficulty chasing their dreams and goals. They may also be reluctant to try new things or learn new skills out of fear or an assumption of failure. This can result in your child isolating themselves, as they may want to avoid being criticized by others. They may also have difficulty setting boundaries with others or saying *no*, as they may feel desperate to please others or get their approval.

If your child has ADHD, it is important to give them as much emotional support and encouragement as possible. Let's look at some ways in which you can help them.

- **Focus on their strengths**: As much as your child may have many difficulties and struggles, there will be things in which they excel. Focus on these things as much as you can. Even if it is something unrelated to their schoolwork, such as having a good sense of humor or being very creative, acknowledging these strengths can help them feel accomplished. Comment on their talents and help them develop them as much as you can.
- **Help them to succeed**: Give your child all the tools they may need to achieve success. If they are writing exams, help them by creating a study schedule for them and finding ways in which they can learn their work easier.
- **Look at their growth**: Never compare your child to others, especially not neurotypical classmates or siblings. Doing this is exceptionally unfair toward your child with ADHD—their brains develop differently and can't be compared to a child whose brain develops typically. Praise the effort your child is putting into their work, whether they achieve the results you may have

wanted them to get or not. Inspire them to grow even more.

- **Discipline things your child does on purpose**: Screaming at or punishing your child for something that their symptoms have caused them to do won't help either of you. When your child misbehaves, ask yourself if they have done that on purpose or if their symptoms have caused them to do it. If their behavior is symptom related, try your best to remain calm. Instead of screaming at them, try using gentle reminders of how their behavior should be or what they should do. If, however, your child lies to you about doing something that they haven't done yet, they should be disciplined. Then you are reprimanding them for lying and not forgetting.

- **Show them love**: Your child may have difficulties building relationships with others. Encourage them to try to make friends at school. Talk to them about what they are struggling with and help guide them to different ways of making friends. While you can't control their ability to make friends, you can show them unconditional love at home. Make them know how important they are and how much you value them.

## ADHD AND DELINQUENT BEHAVIOR, DRUGS, AND SUBSTANCE ABUSE

A decreased sense of self-worth as well as difficulties at school can lead to a variety of delinquent behaviors. Due to their struggles at school, they may be more inclined to drop out. If their ADHD is left untreated, and especially if they suffer from other conditions such as oppositional defiant or conduct disorders as well, they are more likely to have substance abuse issues or engage in risky sexual behaviors.

You can help your child avoid these types of delinquent behaviors by making sure they receive the treatment they need. These treatments can help to increase their concentration, reduce their hyperactivity, and control their impulsive behaviors that often lead to risky actions. Supervise your child at all times, get to know your child's friends, and talk to them about any friends you feel might have a negative impact on them. Make sure that you always know where your child is, who they are with, and that they know you will fetch them if there is ever a problem, or they are under peer pressure to use alcohol or drugs.

Be on the lookout for any signs that your child may be developing these bad habits, and if you ever find them abusing any form of substance, reach out for help immediately. Due to the lack of dopamine their brains develop because of their ADHD, they may get addicted more easily than some of their peers, so it's important to step in sooner rather than later. Always work on your relationship with your child and make sure they are comfortable talking to you about anything. Having open communication in your relationship can lead to your child discussing issues of substance use or peer pressure with you.

As uncomfortable as it may be to discuss sex with your child, it is important to do this from an appropriately early age. Make sure they know the potential risks that being sexually active can bring.

## ADHD AND ANXIETY DISORDERS

Anxiety and ADHD often go hand-in-hand: About 30% of children and 50% of adults with ADHD also suffer from an anxiety disorder (Story, 2017). Having anxiety can result in an inability to concentrate in situations where you feel anxious, leading to difficulty sleeping and insomnia, feeling restless and nervous, and being fearful of impending danger.

If your child has both ADHD and anxiety, the symptoms of both disorders may be more severe. Where concentrating on tasks may have been difficult with ADHD, it can seem impossible when both ADHD and anxiety are present. Let's look at the different forms of anxiety that your child may suffer from.

- **Generalized anxiety disorder**: This is when your child experiences general anxiety about different aspects of their lives or worries about nothing specific. This can include having specific phobias and fears about germs, school, or even certain foods.

- **Social anxiety**: This happens when your child is exceptionally fearful of being in certain social environments or around new people. The anxiety they experience will likely impact how they interact with their peers at school, as they will struggle to form new friendships.

- **Separation anxiety**: This is when a child has extreme worry about leaving their parents—even just for a few minutes—or that something bad might happen to their parents or other important people in their lives.

- **Obsessive-compulsive disorder**: This is when your child has extreme unwanted thoughts (obsessions) and/or repetitive behaviors (compulsions). They normally don't want to have these obsessions or compulsions, but no matter what they do, they can't shake them.

- **Post-traumatic stress disorder**: This happens when your child has experienced some degree of trauma, which can sometimes only set in years afterward. In children, this often manifests after they have been exposed to violence or abuse, or have suffered a severe injury.

If your child ever seems to be overcome by fears and worries, especially if they impact their quality of life, it is important to seek medical help immediately. Your primary care physician or your child's pediatrician should be your first point of contact. They will evaluate your child and make the diagnosis if necessary. There are many different forms of medication, such as antianxiety medicines, that are very effective in reducing anxiety. Your child's doctor may also refer them to a psychologist for therapy, and in severe cases, to a psychiatrist for further and more specialized treatment.

## ADHD AND LEARNING DISABILITIES

Many children with ADHD will also have some sort of learning disability. This is due to the differences in how children with ADHD's brains develop, as their memory, ability to concentrate, how they process sounds and instructions, and how they manage emotions are some of the aspects that are affected by it. This can make learning exceptionally difficult for children with ADHD.

Some of the learning aspects that children with ADHD will often struggle with include

- making rhymes
- sequencing sounds or sentences in the correct order
- sounding out words they don't know
- linking sounds to symbols
- confusing math symbols such as (-) and (+)
- making careless mistakes frequently
- following instructions
- reading with understanding

If your child's learning problems seem more severe, or especially if your child's teacher has picked up on a problem, you should take your child for an evaluation by your general practitioner, child psychologist, or occupational therapist. There are many different types of learning disorders your child might suffer from, including the following:

- **Dyslexia**: Difficulty reading.
- **Dyscalculia**: Difficulty doing math.
- **Dysgraphia**: Problems with writing.
- **Dyspraxia**: Lack of motor skills development.

- **Dysphasia**: Difficulty with understanding, learning, and interpreting language.
- **Auditory processing disorder**: Extreme difficulty understanding instructions.
- **Visual processing disorder**: Problems with how the brain processes visuals.

Treatment for your child's learning disability will depend on the type and severity of the condition. It will usually consist of different techniques for strengthening certain skills and developing learning strategies based on your child's strengths. It is important to treat your child's learning disability and ADHD, as both conditions will exist and cause problems for your child if left untreated.

## ADHD AND DISRUPTIVE MOOD DYSREGULATION DISORDER

Children with ADHD generally struggle to control their emotions due to the slower development of their frontal lobes. This can be even more so when the child also suffers from disruptive mood dysregulation disorder (DMDD). This disorder results in a child being constantly angry, irritable, or annoyed, which often results in severe temper tantrums.

Children with DMDD spend most of their days being annoyed or irritated, and can go into fits of rage for almost no cause or provocation. Something seemingly insignificant, such as cutting a sandwich the wrong way or giving them orange juice instead of mango juice, can result in a fit of rage and screaming that can easily last for more than half an hour. These children tend to be more physically aggressive as well, particularly toward those closest to them, such as their parents or siblings. These fits of rage can be so frequent and extreme that they can disrupt their lives and damage their relationships.

For a diagnosis to be made, these severe temper tantrums should be present at least three or more times a week. The child doesn't have to resort to physical aggression for a diagnosis to be made. Severe verbal fights where it may look like the child is on the brink of becoming physically violent can also be enough to warrant a diagnosis. Once a diagnosis has been made, your child's doctor will recommend treatment options. Often, the medications used for the treatment of ADHD and depression can also be effective for treating DMDD. Therapy such as cognitive behavioral therapy or dialectical behavioral therapy can also help to reduce the impact that your child's DMDD can have on their life and relationships.

## ADHD AND OPPOSITIONAL DEFIANT DISORDER

Oppositional defiant disorder (ODD) is another condition that is often found in children with ADHD: It is present in about 50% of children with combined-type ADHD and in about 25% of children with inattentive-type ADHD (Child Mind Institute, n.d.). This disorder causes children to be defiant, hostile, and uncooperative toward one or more authority figures in their lives. It will often happen that the child will portray ODD toward one parent, typically the parent they spend the most time with, while being caring and loving toward the other parent.

While children with combined or hyperactive-impulsive ADHD may often become defiant while playing with others or even cause unintended or accidental harm to others or themselves, children with ODD's defiance result in an inability to control their tempers. They will blame others for mistakes that they've made, upset or annoy others on purpose, or seem vindictive or spiteful.

If you suspect your child suffers from ODD as well, your general practitioner, mental health specialist, pediatrician, child psychologist, or occupational therapist will do a thorough evaluation to make sure their defiance is caused by this condition and not simply a result of their ADHD.

Once a diagnosis is made, therapy is usually the treatment option of choice. This therapy will often include the parents discovering different ways of dealing with the defiance, as well as teaching the child healthier ways to solve problems. There are also various strategies you can try with your child, for example:

- **Praise the positives**: While your child may have many behavioral traits that can raise your blood pressure, it will help both of you if you try to focus on the positives, no matter how small these positives may seem. Be as specific as possible when you praise them; for example, "I really appreciated how you did your homework today without fighting," or "I'm very proud that you remembered to take your project to school." This will help boost your child's self-confidence and help them realize they are capable of achieving success and that you notice how hard they are trying.
- **Be a role model**: Behave in the way you would want your child to behave. If you don't want your child to lose their temper over seemingly insignificant things, try your best to stay calm. If you want your child to complete their tasks, such as chores, make sure you complete your own. When you spend time with others, behave in a

manner that is socially acceptable so that your child can see and learn how they should behave around others.

- **Pick your battles**: If you react every time your child misbehaves, you will demotivate your child and ruin the relationship you have with them. As much as you may want to rectify every bad behavior your child has, it is important to pick your battles and avoid power struggles.

- **Set boundaries**: Avoid these struggles by setting clear boundaries and giving clear instructions. Find a time when you are both calm to discuss these boundaries and explain to your child why you need to set them. Get their input when you are setting these boundaries. If there is something they feel very strongly about, consider whether you can compromise and adjust the boundary or limit you were planning on setting. By taking their needs and wants into consideration, you will get their buy-in, and they will be much more likely to comply with your boundaries.

- **Create a routine**: Similar to children with ADHD, those with ODD usually react well when they have a strict routine. Include your child in setting this routine so that they feel like they are in charge of their own lives.

- **Spend time together**: If you are the authority figure that your child is defiant toward, your relationship with them has likely been declining. It is important to constantly work on this relationship. One way of doing this is by making time for your child. Do things that your child enjoys. Laugh together. Never disregard the effect that some healthy physical touch, such as a hug, can have on your little one.

- **Be consistent**: There may be times when you feel like you don't have the energy to enforce certain rules, but it is important that you follow through on your rules and boundaries. This way, you will give your child the comfort of knowing what to expect at all times.

- **Give them a chore**: Give them some responsibility in your home by giving them a specific chore to do around the house. Make sure this chore is something that is essential and won't get done if they don't do it. Start out by giving them small chores and then gradually adding to them. Make sure you give them clear instructions on how to complete their chores and praise them when they have successfully completed them. This will give them the confidence to take on bigger tasks without worrying that their ADHD and/or ODD will keep them from achieving success.

- **Be prepared**: When you start introducing these changes in your household, your child may not be cooperative or understand the reasons why specific changes should be implemented. This can cause their behavior to get worse before it gets better. Just stick with it and try to stay calm, even when your child acts out against your new rules and boundaries.

## ADHD AND MOOD DISORDERS

Children with ADHD are more prone to suffering from mood disorders such as depression, dysthymic disorder (chronic low-grade depression), and bipolar disorder. These disorders are more likely to develop during adolescence, and the symptoms can be more severe if the child has never received any treatment for their ADHD.

Although the symptoms of depression can be similar in adults and children, the symptoms of bipolar disorder may present differently in children with ADHD than in adults. While adults will present with periods of distinct and sometimes extreme elation and depression, children will likely experience extreme emotional instability, severe problems socializing with others, and difficulties in their behavior. It can also include periods of psychosis, such as hallucinations and delusions, self-harm, and even suicidal ideation.

Signs of mood disorders you should look out for in your child including

- withdrawing from family members and/or friends.
- a change in appetite, either increasing or decreasing.
- having fears that seem unreasonable.
- irritability.
- a change in academic performance.
- a loss of interest in activities they used to enjoy.
- a change in their sleeping patterns.

Should your child ever show any of these signs, you should keep a close eye on them. If these symptoms continue for more than a few weeks or interfere with their life, it's best to take them to your healthcare professional for an evaluation and potential diagnosis. There are many different treatment options for mood disorders, including antidepressant medication and therapy, whereby a psychologist or psychiatrist will work with your child to discover the cause and pattern of their negative thoughts or depression.

## ADHD AND CONDUCT DISORDER

This mental health disorder occurs when there is a pattern of breaking rules, aggression, being deceitful (such as frequent lying and stealing), and disruptive behavior. It is very common among children with ADHD, particularly those with the combined type of the condition. Some of the signs of conduct disorder in children can include

- bullying their friends.
- threatening or intimidating others.
- being cruel to others or animals.
- being involved in various physical fights.
- using weapons such as bats to hurt others.
- stealing from others.
- forcing others to have sex with them (in older children).
- starting fires to cause damage to property on purpose.
- lying to get things they want.
- running away from home.
- skipping school.

This disorder can be difficult to treat. Firstly, it is important for your child to continue with their treatment for ADHD. This can help reduce their symptoms. Through therapy, your child may learn how to behave around others. As a parent, you can also change the way you interact with your child by choosing a different parenting style. Currently, there are approved medicines to treat conduct disorder.

## ADHD AND TIC DISORDER OR TOURETTE'S SYNDROME

Another mental health illness that children with ADHD are more at risk of getting is Tourette's syndrome, or a tic disorder. With this syndrome, the child will make repeated and involuntary movements or sounds, often referred to as "tics." These can include blinking their eyes, coughing, grunting, sniffing, repeating words or phrases, or moving certain muscles repeatedly. These usually happen several times a day.

Children with ADHD often present with symptoms that may appear to be tics, such as making random noises or fidgeting. The medication your child takes for ADHD may help reduce the symptoms of Tourette's syndrome. This is because their ADHD medicine will improve their ability to pay attention and make them feel calmer. This can help these children control their tics more effectively. Relaxation techniques can also help to reduce a child's tics as well as undergoing therapy, as they will be taught skills on how to better control their tics.

# 4

# CAN CHILDREN WITH ADHD LIVE A NORMAL LIFE?

Understanding how big an impact ADHD can have on your child's life may motivate you to do everything possible to help your child live what would socially be considered a normal life. This may mean considering treatment options you previously never thought you would, and learning new skills through the different forms of therapy available to reduce the symptoms of ADHD.

To help you through this, we will now explore the different treatment options available for treating ADHD and provide tips on how you can help them live a typical life that would be socially acceptable. We will also look at the massive impact that dialectical behavioral therapy can make on your child's life. But first, let's bust a myth that has been going around for many years: Your child can't outgrow ADHD.

## THE POSSIBILITY OF OUTGROWING THEIR SYMPTOMS

Many parents tend to cling to the hope that their children will outgrow their ADHD, as they don't want their children to suffer from these symptoms for the rest of their lives. In children who experience extreme hyperactivity, it may seem as if they are outgrowing their ADHD during adolescence, as this hyperactivity tends to fade away as they grow older. However, significant symptoms still persist in up to 86% of all adults diagnosed with ADHD as children (CHADD 2020).

The good news, however, is that even though symptoms such as disorganization, inattention, and impulsivity often remain lifelong, many teenagers and adults with ADHD have learned how to manage these symptoms more successfully. This can result in their symptoms being much less severe and, together with continuing with their treatment, can result in their ADHD no longer playing a significant role in their lives. This is despite the fact that their brains may still show significant differences from those of neurotypical teenagers or adults.

It is also important to note that many people with inattentive-type ADHD are only diagnosed as adults. Getting this diagnosis as an adult can help them understand why they've been struggling all their lives with concentration and organizational tasks. This busts the myth of outgrowing ADHD even more.

## THE CONSEQUENCES OF IGNORING ADHD

Children with untreated ADHD can face severe consequences, both in their schoolwork and home lives. They will likely get bad grades at school due to their struggles with concentration. If they don't receive the necessary help, they may fall behind, as they won't understand or know everything they are taught. This can lead to children dropping out of school.

They will possibly struggle with regulating their emotions, which can cause major problems in their relationships. They may struggle to make and keep friends. It can be exceptionally tough on children with ADHD when they see how easily their neurotypical peers or even children with treated ADHD may form friendships. This can result in low self-esteem and eventually lead to depression.

The impulsivity that often comes with ADHD can result in more injuries and trips to the emergency room. If ADHD is left untreated, it can increase the child's impulsivity, which can put them at a greater risk of life-threatening injuries.

Untreated ADHD can also lead to a variety of dangerous behaviors, such as

- drinking
- smoking
- eating disorders
- more car accidents once they're old enough to drive
- unsafe sexual practices

## POSSIBILITY OF LIVING A NORMAL LIFE

Even though the symptoms of ADHD can make it more difficult for a child to adjust their behavior to a socially acceptable norm, it is possible for them to have what is often referred to as "a normal life." It might take a lot more work for both the parents and child involved, but the results could be life-changing for your child.

Always keep in mind that your child isn't choosing to behave in a certain way. Their symptoms can make it very difficult to stop what they are doing to consider the consequences of their decisions and behavior. There are various ways in which you can help your child normalize their life as much as possible. This will include making sure your child gets the treatment they need, which can include medication, different forms of therapy, and changing your parenting style.

## AVAILABLE TREATMENTS

Hearing that your child has been diagnosed can be a scary experience, as you will have to make many important decisions, such as what treatment will benefit your child the most. Your child's doctor will recommend a treatment plan, but it can help to ease your nerves enough to make an informed decision if you know what treatments are available, which treatments work best in certain circumstances, and what the potential implications of opting for or against specific treatments may be.

### *Medication*

Most doctors will recommend using medication to treat ADHD in children. Making this decision can be stressful for many parents, as there is a lot of misinformation and misinformed opinion doing the rounds. Discuss these with your child's doctor, as they will quickly be able to explain the pros and cons of all the different medicines.

There are two different types of medication to treat ADHD: Stimulants and nonstimulants. Let's explore these types of medications some more.

### Central Nervous System Stimulants

These are the types of medicines that are most commonly prescribed for ADHD, and work by increasing chemicals such as dopamine and norepinephrine in the child's brain.

This increase in these chemicals will then have a calming effect on the child and help reduce hyperactivity and increase concentration in most children who take it.

The most common central nervous system stimulants that are used to treat ADHD include

- amphetamine-based stimulants, such as Adderall, Dexedrine, and DextroStat.
- dextromethamphetamine, such as Desoxyn.
- dexmethylphenidate, such as Focalin.
- methylphenidate, such as Concerta, Daytrana, Metadate, and Ritalin.

## Nonstimulant Medications

There are also many different nonstimulant medications available to treat your child's ADHD. These are normally considered when the more frequently used stimulants have been unsuccessful in treating ADHD or have caused severe side effects. These are designed to increase the norepinephrine—a chemical that helps with attention and memory—in your child's brain.

The possible non stimulants that may be prescribed include

- atomoxetine such as Strattera.
- antidepressants like nortriptyline.

## Potential Side Effects

As with any other type of medication, both stimulants and non stimulants can cause side effects. If this is the case for your child, their doctor may look at either lowering their dosage or looking at alternative treatments. Severe side effects—such as hallucinations, allergic reactions, high blood pressure, and seizures—are rare. The more common possible side effects can include

- headaches
- difficulty falling and staying asleep
- diarrhea
- nervousness
- irritability
- changes in eating habits, which may lead to weight loss
- dry mouth

Always discuss any concerns you may have about medication with your child's doctor. You should never simply decide to stop treatment without consulting the doctor. They may be able to advise on alternative treatment plans or change the dosage, which can either alleviate side effects or reduce the effects of your child's ADHD. Keep an open mind about the treatment the doctor prescribes, and remember that finding the perfect medication or dosage can take a process of trial and error.

## *Therapy*

Apart from medication, there are various therapy options available that have been known to successfully help those with ADHD manage their symptoms more effectively. These are usually used in conjunction with medication. If your doctor feels that therapy will be effective in treating your child's ADHD, they may refer you to a psychologist or occupational therapist specializing in children with ADHD. Let's look at the different therapy options that may be available for your child.

### Psychotherapy

This form of therapy can help your child come to terms with the symptoms they experience and help them open up about their feelings, thoughts, and difficulties in coping with these symptoms. This can be particularly helpful if your child's symptoms are causing problems with their friendships with their peers and their relationships with authority figures in their life.

Through psychotherapy, the psychologist will help them explore the decisions they make regarding their behavioral patterns. They will then be guided to make healthier choices in how they act around others and bring their behavior to a level that is socially more acceptable.

## Cognitive Behavioral Therapy

This type of therapy forms part of psychotherapy and focuses on changing negative thought processes and reframing your child's thinking about their ADHD symptoms and ways to boost their self-esteem.

It teaches them different ways of coping with difficult symptoms, such as how they can improve their concentration, manage their time more successfully, and avoid procrastination. It also helps them to change any limiting beliefs they may have regarding themselves and their conditions.

## *Other Types of Treatment*

There are many other ways in which you can help your child manage their symptoms more successfully. This can include helping them to learn better social skills, helping them join support groups where they can mingle with others who have the same struggles they do, and changing your parenting style to accommodate your child and their needs.

## Social Skills Training

Since typical ADHD symptoms can make it difficult to adapt to different social circumstances and to behave in a way that is socially acceptable, this type of training can help children build better relationships. Through this training, your child will be helped to understand why the general society regards their behavior as inappropriate and will be guided to change their behavior. They will also be taught how to build stronger relationships with others.

## Support Groups

If there are any support groups in your area for children with ADHD, it can help your child tremendously if they join one. Otherwise, there are various of these groups available online. Being part of these groups can help your child realize that they are not alone and that what they are experiencing is typical for those with ADHD. This can be a huge source of relief for them.

By interacting with other children with ADHD, they may also learn different ways of coping with their struggles and experience a level of empathy that may be difficult for neurotypical people to provide.

## Parenting Skills Training

As important as it is for parents to adapt their parenting styles to suit the needs of their children, it is even more important to do this when your child has a condition like ADHD. Going for training like this can help you better understand your child's behavior and manage it more successfully.

Mindful parent techniques, which we will discuss in great detail later in this book, will help you find better ways to acknowledge positive behavior in your child, discipline your child more effectively, find ways to bond with your little human, help your child strive for and reach success, and manage their stress levels in a more positive way.

## DIALECTICAL BEHAVIORAL THERAPY FOR ADHD

Another very effective form of therapy that's been used more often for the treatment of ADHD is dialectical behavioral therapy (DBT). This form of treatment focuses specifically on the social and emotional challenges a person, particularly those with ADHD, may face in their lives and is extremely efficient for those who are looking for different approaches to the problems they face in their lives.

Initially, DBT was used to treat other forms of mental health conditions, especially those suffering from border-line personality disorder (BPD), where self-harm can be a major problem. Some of the main symptoms of this disorder include severe mood swings, difficulty maintaining relationships, an inability to manage stress, and reckless behavior. Some of the symptoms of BPD can be very similar to those of ADHD.

Since DBT techniques are highly successful in treating emotional turmoil and teaching skills to better regulate emotions, they are also highly effective for those with ADHD. It places a high focus on acceptance, practicing mindfulness, finding the balance between emotional and logical thinking, and self-soothing for successful emotional regulation. One of the various easy ways of doing this is by forcing yourself to have the opposite reactions to how some difficult emotions would typically be dealt with; for example, to smile when you are feeling sad or stay calm when you are in a stressful situation.

What sets DBT apart from other therapeutic methods such as cognitive behavioral therapy is the big focus that is placed on acceptance, not only of the condition that may be present but also of the symptoms and particular emotional difficulties the person may have to deal with. The premise is that once you are able to accept the thoughts and feelings that you are experiencing, change not only seems possible but also probable. Once your child has reached this point, DBT techniques will help them find the balance between this acceptance and the change they would like to see in their lives.

Another major theme in DBT is self-control. The techniques will help your child develop the self-control that will help them bring about the changes they would like to see in their lives. By doing this, they will learn to manage their stress and control their impulsivity more successfully.

DBT is often used in the form of group therapy, as it helps bring home the message that they aren't the only ones suffering due to the symptoms of their ADHD. It can, however, also be implemented on a one-on-one basis.

## HOW DIALECTICAL BEHAVIORAL THERAPY WORKS

DBT is made up of four different modules, and to reap the maximum benefits from the techniques learned during this form of therapy, it is important that equal focus be placed on all four of these modules. Together, they are designed to improve how a person, or in this case, your child, can control and manage their behavior, emotions, and thoughts. Let's look at these four modules and how they can help your child:

- **Mindfulness**: Your child will learn to be present at the moment and focus only on what is happening in the now, without fear or worry about the future. Doing this can help your child to calm down, as they will reduce their thoughts, fears, and emotions about what may happen in the future, while only paying attention to what they are busy with and how they should care for themselves at that moment.

- **Distress tolerance**: This will help your child in managing their emotions more successfully in difficult times. Your child will learn healthy ways of soothing themselves and, as a result, will be able to avoid explosive emotional outbursts.

- **Interpersonal effectiveness**: This is about focusing on their needs in relationships, as well as healthy and effective ways of making sure their needs are met. A big focus here is placed on respect, not only for themselves but also for the people in their lives. They will be taught how to listen effectively and talk to others in a way that shows this respect. Possibly most importantly, they will learn how to set boundaries and say *no* to others in a respectful but necessary way.

- **Emotional regulation**: Your child will learn to manage their emotions more effectively without acting on the over-the-top feelings they may have. This will help them to stay calm during difficult times.

Over the next few chapters, we will explore how you can use the skills that are taught in DBT in the daily parenting of your child, taking a mindful approach when dealing with your child, and helping them grow into the type of adults you would want to spend time with.

# 5

# NECESSARY YET MINDFUL PARENTING SKILLS

We've already touched briefly on how becoming more mindful as a parent can help your child. Now, let's delve into this a bit deeper by exploring how you can go about doing this.

In this chapter, we will look at what mindful parenting entails and the massive impact it can have on your child. We will then explore how you can use the key factors of mindful parenting to become your child's biggest cheerleader. Lastly, I will give you proven tips on how to make changes to your parenting style to be more mindful with your child and help them deal with their daily struggles.

## WHAT IS MINDFUL PARENTING?

Life can get busy for most parents. You have to juggle your work, responsibilities at home, your children and their schoolwork, and often other family members and friends who require some of your time. It can become a mad rush to get everything done and for your children to be fed and in bed at a decent time. For many parents, the frustrations of rushing through their tasks can result in yelling at their children for not complying or taking too long, only for guilt to set in once the kids are asleep.

This can feel like it's on steroids when you have a child with ADHD who may, at times, even seem spiteful in their behavior. This is why mindful parenting can be so effective, not only in calming your life down but also by viewing your life (and your children) with acceptance and without any judgment.

As I've mentioned, mindfulness is about being present in the moment. It has been practiced for centuries as the basis of Buddhist meditation. The purpose of mindful parenting is to calm yourself down before you simply react to your child's behavior and carefully consider their actions, the causes of their behavior, and how you should react to them. It is about accepting yourself and your child and improving the relationship you have with your little one.

A common misconception about mindful parenting is that you should never discipline your child or that you will allow your child to walk all over you. In reality, this isn't the case. As much as mindful parenting may result in you reacting more positively, you will still have rules in place and discipline your child when they misbehave or break these rules. However, while you might have resorted to shouting and severely punishing your child in the past, mindful parenting is about not allowing your emotions to get the better of you. By being more mindful, you will be able to better control your reaction.

## WHY MINDFUL PARENTING IS CRUCIAL FOR ADHD CHILDREN

By staying calm in times of difficulty, mindful parenting can help to improve your and your child's resilience and overall well-being. This parenting style is designed to make the difficulties in life easier to manage. You will model the behavior you would like to see in your child and, over time, build positive skills in both you and your child. Many of these skills will be opposite to the symptoms most commonly experienced by children with ADHD, for example the following

- attention (as opposed to distractibility and lack of concentration)

- being aware (as opposed to living like they are on autopilot)
- becoming responsive (as opposed to reacting in a negative way)
- being intentional (as opposed to going with the motions)
- problem-solving (as opposed to relying on bad habits to get out of a sticky situation)
- compassion and respect (as opposed to criticism and impatience)

These benefits can drastically improve your child's ability to deal with the symptoms of ADHD, which will not only make life easier for you and your little one but also improve their mental well-being. You will be able to help them see ADHD for what it is: A mental condition that doesn't define who they are. This can help them to accept ADHD as being only a small part of their life, not something that has to control every aspect of them.

Helping a child manage the symptoms of their ADHD can be a difficult task that will require you to be flexible, resilient, and responsive. It is not something that can happen overnight, and since you've been programmed all your life to act in a certain way, it can be difficult to find joy during stressful times. Practicing mindfulness can make this easier for you, as you will only focus on the present moment and what should happen instead of thinking about how many times you've tried to assist your child with the same problem or how many times you may still have to do it.

Being more mindful in your parenting can help create a space where your child feels comfortable and safe. If you make a conscious effort not to judge your child for their symptoms, your child will realize that you are trying to help them, which will give them more confidence to do the same. You can also help other family members and siblings by following your example. If they feel safe at home and in their relationship with them, they will be more comfortable discussing their struggles with you. If they know you will hear them out, no matter what the problem is or what they want to discuss with them, they will open up about the big and small things in their life.

Mindful parenting will help you to identify small issues before they potentially become big problems. By being more mindful when your child talks to you about small, everyday occurrences, you will also be able to pick up on and address something sooner rather than later. You will become a more focused listener, and by hearing and understanding exactly what your child is saying to you, you will know how to respond. Since children with ADHD will, in general, have more obstacles in their lives that they will need to overcome, you can help them tremendously by tackling small issues before they become big.

You will also be able to notice behavioral changes in your child much sooner. As I've mentioned in Chapter 3, many people with ADHD will at some point in their lives also be diagnosed with another mental health disorder. By being more present at the moment, you may see signs of other mental health concerns in your child before they fully manifest. Look at how your child is behaving and try to see if there are specific triggers to their outbursts. Even if they don't have any other health concerns, knowing what triggers them will be a massive help in helping them to control their emotions and outbursts. This will not only help your child at home but also at school, where their ADHD is likely causing challenges for their teacher as well. If you can help your child through their triggers and outbursts, they will be able to manage these better while in class as well.

Due to the symptoms a child with ADHD usually has, they tend to get on their parents' nerves a lot more than a neurotypical child would. This can result in more fights at home as their child, often due to their controllable symptoms, is not doing what their parents expect them to do. If the parents feel overwhelmed by their own stresses, they may give in to their child's demands more than they would like to, which can result in even more behavioral problems as the child will realize that if they continue with their troublesome behavior for long enough, they will get their way. However, if you practice more mindfulness, you will focus only on the stress that you have in the moment, not worry about what might happen in the future. This can help you to control your frustrations with your child better, which will help you to reprimand your child in a healthier way.

The longer you continue parenting your child more mindfully and successfully, the better your relationship with your child will be. Over time, your child will see that you treat them fairly and that they are loved and appreciated. This will improve their self-esteem, help them to feel understood, and result in them making more of an effort to improve their behavior. This will also help to reduce the stress that your child is experiencing and, as a result, improve their mental well-being.

## KEY FACTORS OF MINDFUL PARENTING

Even though mindful parenting is largely focused on three aspects, namely paying attention to the present moment, making the effort to understand the behavior of your child, and being non-judgmental, compassionate, and accepting, there is a lot more to it. Let's look at the specific skills—or key factors, if you will—that can help you ace your role as a mindful parent:

- **Listening**: The key to listening as a mindful parent is to listen to understand, not to respond. It is about taking in everything your child is saying to you and making sure you understand what they mean before you respond. It can take a lot of patience and practice; it can take numerous tries before you are able to really master the skill of listening with attention. When listening to your child, take in your environment. You may soon realize that specific sounds or smells may trigger certain thoughts and emotions in your child.

- **Acceptance**: This doesn't just extend to your child and their thoughts and feelings, but also to yourself. To do this, you may have to let go of any unrealistic expectations and/or limiting beliefs you may have about your child and yourself as a parent. It is likely that you have made many mistakes in the past. Accept this and stop judging yourself. Holding on to things that may have happened won't help you or your child build the future and the relationship you both deserve. Similarly, accept without judgment and forgive your child for their past. Focus on the present moment and how you can use what you now know and understand to better handle the situations.

- **Emotional awareness**: Become aware of all the emotions that are involved—yours and your child's. Carefully consider what your child is feeling at the moment and discuss these emotions with them. Similarly, become deliberate about the emotions you show your child. Identify your own emotions, the cause of these emotions, and whether these are the types of emotions you want to show your child. If it isn't, take a moment to calm yourself down and help your child to also cool off. Don't allow negative or unnecessary emotions to control your parenting style or your relationship with your child.

- **Self-regulation**: This ties in with becoming more aware of your own feelings. The more you become aware of your emotions and whether these are the emotions you would like to portray to your child, the quicker you will be able to regulate yourself. This can help you change some of your automatic behaviors, such as yelling at your child when they make you angry or punishing them immediately when they are misbehaving without considering what the cause of their actions may be. Practicing better self-regulation will help you to think before you act so that you can avoid overreacting.

- **Compassion**: It's a fact that you won't always agree with your child's actions, feelings, or thoughts. Despite this, it is important that you always treat your child with compassion. This involves trying your best to understand their point of view, being empathetic towards them, and doing what you can to help them without passing judgment. Also, have compassion for yourself. Stop blaming yourself if a situation doesn't turn out the way you had hoped it would. Leave the past where it belongs: In the past. Focus on the present and try to be better the next time you're faced with a similar situation.

The more you practice mindfulness in your parenting, the easier it will become. Soon, you may even realize that your and your child's mental well-being has improved, as mindful parenting is known to reduce stress, depression, and anxiety in both the child and the parent. One of the reasons for this is the improved relationship you will have with your child.

## BE YOUR CHILD'S BIGGEST CHEERLEADER

Everyone needs to have someone in their corner that they know will have their back no matter what happens. For a child, it is important that this person be a parent, as this will help them to feel safe and secure in their homes and in their relationship with the person who is supposed to love them unconditionally.

You can be their biggest cheerleader by helping them through their struggles, giving them advice when needed, guiding them to make the best decisions, and supporting them in their dreams and goals. When you parent a child with ADHD, you may find that these dreams and goals change weekly. This can be extremely frustrating, as you may spend money helping them get the equipment they need for a specific activity, only for them to change their mind and not be interested in this activity anymore.

As infuriating as this can be, try to stay calm and patient with your child. Try to motivate your child to push through with the activity for a little longer, and if this doesn't help to spark their interest, don't force them to do something they don't want to do. You can always sell the equipment you've bought again secondhand, and ultimately, your child's happiness and ability to chase their dreams are more important than the few dollars you may have wasted. Eventually, they will find your passion and know that you've done everything you can to help them get there.

Also, as they are jumping between activities, try to look for the silver lining instead of working yourself up. Comment on their amazing sense of adventure and courage to try different things. Their ADHD symptoms may motivate them to take on activities that others would be too hesitant to do. Praise them for this instead of breaking them down for constantly jumping between activities or even attempting things that you may consider to be too risky.

Apart from allowing them to chase their dreams, knowing that you are there for them will also help to teach them not to take life too seriously. Since people with ADHD are more likely to be diagnosed with other mental health disorders, it is important that they learn from a young age to have fun and that they are capable of achieving greatness. Giving them the opportunity to try different activities that they are interested in or enjoy doing can help them improve their mental wellness and teach them valuable lessons on how to manage their stress levels more successfully.

You can also look at making the current chores they have, which they might hate doing, more fun. If they don't want to clean their room, turn it into a fun game; for example, you can let them do a speed rush where they can try to see how quickly they can clean their room. Make time to be silly with your child. Let them spend some carefree moments with your child, even if it is only for a few minutes at a time. Laugh together as often as you can to strengthen the bond.

I've said it again, but it's important to always be patient with your child. Even if it doesn't seem like it, your child is likely trying their best. Recognize the efforts that they are making. A pat on the back will mean a lot more to them than pointing fingers.

## HOW TO MINDFULLY PARENT YOUR CHILD THROUGH ADHD

Practicing mindfulness can seem overwhelming, and you may not even know where to start. The good news is that you don't have to change your entire life to be more mindful in your parenting styles. Apart from the tips we've already looked at, there are many other different things you can start to implement immediately, to mention only a few:

- **Breathe**: If you are feeling stressed or like you may lose your temper with your child, practice deep breathing techniques to help you calm down. Breathe in through your nose for four seconds, hold your breath for two seconds, exhale through your mouth for four seconds, and hold again for two seconds. Repeat this as often as you need to until you have cooled off. Teach these breathing techniques to your child as well. Doing this together will not only help you both to settle but can also be a great bonding moment.

- **Meditate**: Deep breathing forms an important part of meditation, but you can increase your focus on being present even more by using this ancient Buddhist practice. There are many different ways in which you can meditate, and there are also videos and courses online that teach you this technique. However, you can keep it as simple as you need to.
- Find a quiet place where you can sit comfortably.
- Decide how much time you want to spend meditating. Set a timer accordingly. This will help you to know when you've reached your chosen limit and allow you to focus on your meditation without wondering when you should stop.
- Do your deep breathing exercises and focus only on your breathing. As thoughts enter your mind, accept these thoughts without judgment and turn your focus back to your breathing. Accepting that you have these thoughts can make it easier to move on from them.
- Pay attention to your other senses as you experience specific thoughts. This can help you figure out how you truly feel about certain things or events.

- Once your timer goes off, spend some time reflecting on your meditation session by accepting your thoughts and how relaxed your body feels.
- **Decide on acceptable behaviors**: Help your child manage their behavior and impulses better by discussing which types of behaviors are acceptable and which are not. Consider your child's wishes and needs when you determine what you will allow going forward. Having these discussions can require a lot of patience and empathy, but once the rules have been set, it will relieve a lot of the stress you and your child may experience as you will both know what can and shouldn't happen, and what type of behavior will be disciplined. If your child has specific behavioral habits that you're willing to live with, allow them these freedoms. Try not to limit them too much. As their behavior improves, you can gradually look at addressing more behaviors.
- **Define the rules**: Once you and your child are both aware of what would be considered acceptable, it is important that you're consistent in following through. You can't allow something that has been considered inappropriate one day and not allow it the next. This will only cause confusion. Consider posting the rules

somewhere in the house where all the family members can see them. This will remind everyone daily of what is expected.

- **Reward good behavior**: Consider some form of a reward system. If your child is still young, a simple sticker chart can work. As they get older, you can reward your child's good behavior by allowing them more privileges, such as screen time or tokens they can eventually exchange for pocket money. This will not only help to reward good behavior but also discourage negative ones.

- **Manage aggression**: Emotional and aggressive outbursts are often typical for children with ADHD. These can be exceptionally difficult to deal with, so it is important that you try to remain as calm as possible during these outbursts. Reacting to their aggression with your own won't help either of you. Creating a time-out can be effective for both of you. Explain to your child that this time-out is not to punish them but rather to allow you both a few minutes to cool off before continuing the conversation. During this time, your child can consider their behavior, and you can think about how you can guide them to behave in a more appropriate manner. No matter how difficult it may be, it can be helpful to try to ignore mildly disruptive behavior, as this can be a way for your child to reduce some of the stress they may be experiencing. Or try to find a healthier way to help them release their stress. Make sure the behavior you may decide to allow falls within the rules you have decided to approve.

- **Create smaller goals**: Difficult tasks can seem extremely overwhelming to children with ADHD. One way of helping them to do this would be to break their tasks down into smaller, more manageable goals. Using a calendar and schedule that are easily accessible can help your child keep track of their tasks. Color coding their chores and schoolwork can also help to reduce the overwhelm they may experience when they are looking at their calendar.

- **Organize your child's life**: Help your child create organization in their lives by removing as much chaos as possible. Work on keeping your home clean and neat so that your child will always know where to find something or how to put things in their place. This can help them to focus more on the task at hand. It can also help to create specific areas in your home where your child will do homework. Make sure this space is as free from distraction as possible, as this will help them increase their focus.

- **Reduce distractions**: Apart from finding a place where your child can do homework without distractions, try to remove more things that can take their focus off the task at hand. As your child gets older, it is important that you help them by limiting their screen time, as spending too much time in front of the television or playing video games can increase the amount of built-up energy in your child, making them more susceptible to distractions and acting on their impulses.

- **Encourage exercise**: Help your child get rid of some of their built-up energy by allowing plenty of time for physical activity. This can also help your child to place their focus on their movements. Physical exercise can help to reduce their impulsivity and concentration and can give their mental wellness a boost. The hyperfocus these children often experience can help them focus their energy on practicing the sport of their choice, helping them to excel.

- **Create healthy sleep patterns**: Sleep is very important for all people, but especially for children with ADHD. However, many children with this condition can struggle to settle at night and fall asleep. This is largely due to their inattention, hyperactivity, and impulsiveness.

You can help your child create the healthiest sleeping pattern possible by reducing stimulants such as sugar and caffeine shortly before bed, and reducing screen time for at least an hour before bedtime. The blue light that is produced by screens reduces a person's ability to produce melatonin, the hormone responsible for helping a person fall asleep.

- **Encourage out-loud thinking**: Many children with ADHD struggle with self-control, which can result in them behaving and speaking in a manner that may seem impulsive and disruptive to others. You can help your child through this by asking them to explain their thoughts before they act on them. Talking about this out loud can help you understand how they reason, which can then help you guide them to behave in a way that is socially more acceptable.

- **Let them pause**: Apart from verbalizing their thoughts, you can help your child be less disruptive and impulsive by teaching them to wait a minute or two before responding or acting. This minute of pausing can help them to rethink their actions, calm down, and react in a manner that is more appropriate.

- **Take breaks**: No person can work nonstop without taking breaks. This is even more important for a child with ADHD. If you force them to work without taking proper breaks, you will increase the feeling of overwhelm and frustration they may experience. Using timers can be very helpful in doing this. If you see that your child can concentrate for 45 minutes, set the timer. Once the time has passed, set another timer for 15 minutes and allow them a break. It can help to use an analog clock for this, as this can visually help your child understand how much time has passed and how long they still need to work.

- **Spend time outside**: When your child is on a break, allow them to go outside whenever possible. Spending time outside in the sun can help to increase your child's release of dopamine, which can then help them to improve their focus once they get back to their tasks. If you have a backyard, let them run around or take them for a walk in your neighborhood. This way, they not only get their dopamine boost, but they will also get rid of some of their energy by being physically active.

- **Seek help**: There may be times when you or your child need encouragement. Always remember that there is no shame in seeking help. Your doctor may be able to refer your child to a child psychologist or occupational therapist who can help find the cause of your and your child's symptoms and suggest ways in which you can help your child. This therapist can also help reduce your child's stress and anxiety.

Understanding how mindful parenting can help improve your and your child's lives, as well as the relationship you have with your child, is an important first step in helping your child manage their symptoms of ADHD more successfully. Once you have become used to being more mindful, you can start to include techniques taught in DBT in your parenting.

6

# DIALECTICAL BEHAVIORAL THERAPY SKILLS AND MINDFULNESS ACTIVITIES

Being more mindful in your parenting is a good start to better managing your child's symptoms of ADHD. If you incorporate the skills and techniques taught in DBT, you will up your parenting game to a new level and likely have a calmer and more cooperative child.

Mindfulness is one of the four pillars of DBT. We have already looked at how you can become more mindful. Now, we will explore some exercises that can help your child be more present in the moment. We will also look at the other three pillars of DBT—interpersonal effectiveness, distress tolerance, and emotional regulation—and how you can help your child practice them. Then, we will discuss more exercises you can help your child with that can help reduce the severity of their symptoms.

## MINDFULNESS

As we have discussed, mindfulness is all about being present and focusing only on what you're doing at that moment. It is about accepting yourself without judgment. There are various exercises your child can do that will help them become more mindful so that they can reduce the overwhelm their symptoms may cause them to feel. These exercises will only take a few minutes at a time and will be well worth the time spent on them, particularly if your child struggles with managing stressful situations and the challenges that their symptoms may cause in their daily life.

### *Take a Seat*

This can be seen as the child version of meditation, as your child will spend a few minutes focusing on what they are feeling to regulate how they should react, as well as what might be causing distractions. This one is easy for even younger children to remember, as it is built around the acronym *SEAT*. In the beginning, it can be best for your child to do these exercises while sitting or lying down in a quiet, relaxing environment. However, as they get more comfortable with this exercise, they will be able to do it in any environment, even in class surrounded by their friends:

- **Sensations**: How is your child's body feeling? Do they have any aches? What are they hearing? What are they smelling? Let them use all their senses to identify what is happening in their bodies.

- **Emotions**: What is your child feeling? Are they happy or sad? Are they showing any signs of nervousness or anxiety? Are they calm? If it is possible, let them name the emotion they are feeling most strongly.

- **Actions**: What action does your child want to take? What action do they need to take? Is there a difference between their wants and needs? What is the difference? How will they go about choosing what to do? What will the consequences of their choice be?

- **Thoughts**: What is your child thinking about? They can explore all the thoughts that are popping into their heads by understanding them, accepting them without any judgment, and then moving on to the next thought.

In the beginning, encourage your child to do this exercise at least once a day or every time they feel like they are under pressure. Eventually, checking in with themselves by quickly doing this exercise will become second nature and can lead them to make much better decisions.

## *Hot Chocolate Breath*

This is a breathing exercise that is easy for children of all ages to do. Doing this can help them to calm down, overcome the limitations that their self-consciousness and low self-esteem may bring, and focus on the choices and actions they need to take. This exercise uses basic visualization and can be done virtually anywhere:

- Let your child cup their hands in front of their faces as if they are holding a cup of hot chocolate. If your child prefers another hot beverage, such as tea, they can swap the hot chocolate out for that, but the idea is that it must be something hot.
- Let them visualize holding the cup and smelling the hot chocolate by inhaling deeply through their nose.
- Next, let them blow out as if they are blowing their hot chocolate (or cup of tea) cool.
- Let your child repeat this visualization for a minute or two, smelling the hot chocolate by inhaling through their nose, and blowing the hot chocolate to cool down by exhaling through their mouth.
- Allow your child to settle into their own rhythm while doing this breathing exercise.

Connecting their breathing to something that they really enjoy, such as drinking hot chocolate, can help them feel more positive about their struggles. If they are feeling positive, they are more likely to be able to focus on what they want to achieve and avoid distractions.

### Stop Sign

This technique is a great way for your child to start and end their day. It relies on having a visual cue to get the exercise started. A stop sign is often used, as it literally tells your child to stop what they are busy doing and regain control over their emotions and thoughts, but you can use any form of visual cue that will work for your child. Print a couple of these out and put them up in places around your home where you want your child to focus or take a moment to regain control. You can also make smaller signs that your child can keep in their school bags to take out whenever they are feeling overwhelmed at school:

- Every time your child sees the chosen visual cue, such as the stop sign, they should follow the command and stop whatever they were doing.
- Let them take a long, deep breath through their nose. Exhale deeply all the way, hold their breath for a few seconds, and repeat the process.
- Once they settle into a breathing rhythm, let them observe their surroundings, bodies, and

thoughts. Let them ask themselves questions such as, "What is happening right now?" "What am I thinking?" or "How am I feeling?"

- Once they have checked in with themselves, they can continue with their day.

This technique may seem very simple, but it is very effective in helping a child with ADHD identify their distractions, understand what is happening in their lives, and avoid their impulses.

### *The Silent Sigh*

Chances are, your child often sighs when they are frustrated, annoyed, overwhelmed, or when you ask them to do something that they don't want to do. As much as it can be irritating when your child sighs all the time, it actually has a psychological purpose: To calm the body down. The good news is that you can actually use your child's signs to be more mindful:

- When they feel like their stress is getting too much for them, let them exhale as if they were sighing and clear their lungs of any air.
- Let them close their eyes while doing this so that they can focus only on what is causing their stress or frustration.

- If they need to, they can repeat these silent signs a couple of times until they feel more in control of their emotions and bodies.

By the time they have finished this exercise, they should be calm enough to start considering different ways they can solve their problems and, as a result, feel less overwhelmed or annoyed.

## *Zoom in Sounds*

Many children with ADHD will only focus on certain things and completely disregard the rest. This is particularly evident when you give a child with ADHD instructions to follow. They will often only hear a section of the instruction and then get the outcome of the command completely wrong, much to the dismay of their parents. By helping them become more mindful of sounds, you can help them improve their listening skills and, as a result, their ability to follow instructions. In the beginning, your child will need your assistance to do this exercise, but as they become more equipped at controlling their focus, they will be able to do it by themselves:

- Let your child sit up straight with their eyes closed.

- Make some sort of short, melodic sound, such as by ringing a bell, playing a cord on a guitar, or hitting a note or two on the piano.
- Let them listen closely so that they are able to identify the beginning, middle, and end of the sound. Let them explain how every part sounds.
- Once the sound fades, let them identify a distant sound they can hear, such as a car driving past or the wind blowing.
- Next, let them identify a close sound, such as a sibling playing in another room, the fridge, or a clock ticking.
- Once they have identified a nearby noise, let them focus only on your voice. Talk to them about the sounds they have identified.
- After a few moments, turn their attention to the sound of their own breathing. Let them sit like this for a while before finishing this exercise.

Focusing on specific sounds is not only a great way for your child to improve their listening abilities but also to eliminate distractions. This can be particularly handy when your child must write exams in a room filled with other students. They can narrow their focus from sounds they hear outside, to the normal classroom noises, to the question paper in front of them.

## INTERPERSONAL EFFECTIVENESS

This pillar of DBT is about their wants, needs, and roles in the relationships in their lives, with a major focus on having respect for themselves and the people in their lives. It is about improving the way they communicate with others and setting boundaries that will protect them in difficult times. Improving their interpersonal effectiveness will also go a long way toward reducing the negative and limiting thoughts and emotions your child may have, not only toward themselves but also the people in their lives.

To practice this, you can help your child with various exercises based on three acronyms: *THINK*, *FAST*, and *GIVE*. Let's look at each of these exercises, how you can help your child with them, and what your child may gain from doing them.

### *Think*

This exercise is all about working through negative emotions you may experience and how you can reduce them. This exercise is particularly handy when your child is struggling with their relationships with others or feeling upset over something someone did. Let's look at this acronym and how you can help your child with this:

- **Think**: Help your child to carefully consider the situation they are in, not just from their perspective but also the viewpoint of the other person involved. Ask your child why they are reacting in a specific way and what they think the other person may be thinking. This can help them realize that just as they believe the other person is being deliberate or unreasonable, the other person can think the exact same of them.

- **Have empathy**: Once your child has determined what the other person may be thinking, ask them what they believe the other person may be feeling. Ask them how they would feel if someone treated them the way your child may have. Let them empathize with the other person.

- **Interpretations**: Help your child understand what the possible reasons are for how the other person treated them. If your child struggles to think of these reasons by themselves, give suggestions to help their thought processes. It can help to start with the most ridiculous suggestions and then work your way to the more realistic ones. If you start out with outlandish reasons, the more realistic ones can seem less bad for your child.

- **Notice**: Help your child to pay attention to the action and body language of the other person. That person may act brave but might actually be scared. Ask your child to take in everything that has happened by asking them open-ended questions about their interaction with this person. Also, keep an eye out for any signs that the other person may make an effort to solve the problem and salvage the relationship.

- **Kindness**: Help your child to show compassion and kindness to the other person in their response. Explain to your child that being nice to the other person doesn't mean they need to necessarily forgive and forget, and that showing kindness is most certainly not a sign of weakness. If they are too upset about the situation to be kind, help them to create some space. They can tell the other person that they need some space before they can discuss the problem or that they need time to think. No matter what the situation is, reacting with kindness is always better than resorting to name-calling.

The exercise around the acronym *THINK* is not only a valuable tool to improve their interpersonal effectiveness, but can also be used in distress tolerance, which we will discuss later on in this chapter. Going over these steps will help them to control the emotions they may experience toward the other person and, as a result, manage their relationships much better.

## *Fast*

Practicing this exercise will help your child handle conflict with respect, not just for themselves but for others as well. The acronym for this exercise is *FAST*, and it will help your child feel good about themselves and keep their dignity, no matter how the conflict ends; even if the conflict doesn't end in their favor, they will know that they kept their dignity throughout the process:

- **Fair**: Help your child to handle every situation they may find themselves in with fairness, both toward themselves and the other person involved, as well as with their emotions, thoughts, and actions. Being fair will help your child avoid judgment and instead look for the reason behind the conflict. Your child will try to understand the situation and discover what the truth might be before they simply react. They will no longer feel powerless in conflict situations, but rather be empowered by knowing how to react.

- **Apologies**: Assist your child to know when they should apologize, avoid apologizing simply because they think they need to, and word their apologies in such a way that they take ownership for the things they've done or said that were wrong. Listen to your child when they tell you what happened. Make sure you understand and ask your child about what they believe the other person's point of view was. If your child was in the wrong, help them word their apology. If they haven't done anything wrong, help them to understand this so that they can stand their ground.

- **Stick to their values**: Your child should stand up for what they believe in, but you can help them do it in such a way that they don't offend anyone or cause unnecessary fights. Help your child determine what they value in life and allow them to be honest. Even if you don't agree with their values, they are entitled to their own opinions and feelings. If you can help them, make a list of their values and what is important to them, they will know how to react in a future conflict situation by respecting their own values.

- **Truthful**: Ask your child to always be truthful with you and others. Exaggerating or minimizing a situation won't help them understand their problems or how they can manage their symptoms of ADHD in such a way that they can solve their problems and resolve their conflicts in a more manageable way. If your child remains honest and truthful at all times, they will not only keep their own respect but also gain the respect of others.

Once your child gets used to using both the fast and slow methods of exercising, they may even be able to use them in conjunction, which can be a vital tool in the way they build and maintain relationships and communicate with others.

### Give

The final interpersonal skill you can help your child learn is built on the acronym *GIVE*. This will help them communicate with others in all types of situations, from conflict situations to friendly conversations. Give forms the foundation for all their communication and relationships.

- **Gentle**: Help your child to always be gentle when they are interacting with other people. This is not just being mindful of their own emotions and thoughts but also those of others. When they are able to do this, they will show the other person that they are understood and loved instead of feeling attacked. This will help to make the other person more approachable in their communication with your child, which can lead to better outcomes for both parties involved.

- **Interested**: Encourage your child to pay attention to what others are saying, just like they want others to listen to them. Help them understand that body language can play a big role in this: Tell them to face the person they are talking to, make eye contact, and say words like "oh," "really," or "uh-huh" to show they are listening and not to cross their arms. Remind your child that by showing interest in what the other person is saying, they will be encouraging them to communicate more openly with your child.

- **Validate**: Help your child make sure they are understanding the other person correctly by paraphrasing what was said in their own words; for example, "So, what you mean is..." Also, encourage your child to validate the other person's feelings by echoing them back to them. If the other person is telling your child about something that is very frustrating to them, your child can react by saying something such as, "I would also be upset by this." This will help the other person feel like your child cares about them and what they are saying.

- **Easy-going**: When a person is interacting with someone else, it is important to appear as easy-going, comfortable, and relaxed as possible.

Explain to your child how this can make them seem more approachable, which will help them build stronger relationships with other people.

Following these skills will help your child be more effective in their interpersonal interactions, deal with conflict easier, maintain respect for others and for themselves, and experience less stress in their relationships with others.

## DISTRESS TOLERANCE

Your child's emotions can, at times, get so overwhelming that they may struggle to control themselves. This can result in behavior that may make certain situations seem unbearable, not just for your child but also for you as the parent. It can also lead them to act more on their impulses and, as a result, lead them to make some bad decisions.

This is where distress tolerance training comes in. These techniques are designed to distract your child from the difficult emotions they are experiencing, which can make it easier for them to deal with these difficult situations. Apart from this, your child will realize that by accepting their difficult situation and themselves, they will be able to handle these struggling times easier. Let's look at some ways in which you can help your child achieve this.

## Make a Change

Let them put their bodies in charge and change what they are doing. If they are sitting down, let them walk around. If they are inside, let them spend some time outside. By following their bodies, they would change their focus from their emotions to their bodies and how they are moving.

## Have Fun

Allow them to do something they really enjoy doing, not what they have to do. If they're having a meltdown because they are struggling with homework, let them have a 15-minute break (even if it isn't time for a break yet) and allow them to play a game or go for a walk. If you force them to continue with their work while they're in such a state, they won't get anything done in any way. Just keep a close eye on this to make sure your child doesn't come to abuse this allowance of extra free time in the future.

## Help Out

Helping others can be a valuable tool in reducing times of distress. This can provide your child with a purpose in their life and help them view their role in the world in a different way. Look at your child's interests and find out if there is a charity organization in your area where your child can volunteer; for example, an animal shelter. If they are too young to physically help out, they might look at acquiring food donations for the animals. Find ways in which your child can feel like they have a purpose.

### *Make a Comparison*

Ask your child to think of a time when they weren't feeling as overwhelmed and emotionally distressed. Guide their thoughts to how they were able to overcome this the previous time they had a similar difficulty. Praise them for the success they were able to achieve and, maybe more importantly, let them praise themselves for it. This will help them realize that since they have been able to overcome these challenges in the past, they will be able to do so again.

### *Look at the Opposites*

When your child is experiencing an overwhelmingly negative emotion, help them to think of what the complete opposite emotion would be; for example, if they are furious, the opposite might be elation. Then, let them do something that can bring them closer to this opposite emotion, such as watching funny video clips online. Once they are able to bring themselves out of difficult emotions by themselves, they will have learned a skill that will benefit them for the rest of their lives.

### *Think Big*

When your child is going through a distressing time, help them to eliminate these negative thoughts by filling their minds with other big ideas and thoughts. Please help them include as much detail as possible in these thoughts. This can be anything from how they would love to redecorate their rooms to guessing what all their friends are doing.

### *Self-Soothing*

Many people use this technique to help themselves calm down by using all their senses: sight, sound, smell, touch, and taste. A child with ADHD may feel overwhelmed when they have to bring in all these senses while they are in a distressing situation, so you can help them by simplifying this technique for them. Ask them how they would try to comfort a friend who is experiencing a similar situation. Then, help them to apply the same techniques they would use with a friend to themselves to bring comfort.

While distress tolerance is largely based on flipping negative emotions into positive ones or distracting the child from the negativity, this will be a lot easier if your child is able to manage their emotions in a more successful way.

## EMOTIONAL REGULATION

The successful management of emotions is key for all people, and particularly so for children with ADHD as well as their parents. Since these young ones will struggle with regulating their feelings, their behavior can appear to be extremely over the top at times. Also, your child's resultant explosive behavior can cause your emotions to run haywire with you, causing unnecessary tension and fights in the home. Although most of the DBT exercises discussed already can help with controlling emotions more effectively, let's look at some specific ones to help with emotional regulation.

### *Label the Emotions*

One proven way of managing emotions is by naming them as you or your child feel them. By doing this, you realize that what you are feeling is simply an emotion that you can control, and as a result, you can decide that you don't want this emotion to take control of your body. For example, if you are feeling worked up over your child not doing what they are supposed to do, you can tell yourself, "I'm feeling frustrated by the situation. Acting on my frustrations will only make things worse. I won't allow this." Similarly, your child may be upset that they can't have more screen time. They can then say to themselves,

"I'm sad that I can't watch another show. Crying over it won't help anyone or let me continue to watch my show."

Saying the name of the emotion out loud can help you and your child come to terms with it easier, as your brain reacts differently to something that is thought than to something that is heard. Also, by pausing to identify the emotion, you or your child are giving yourselves a timeout and a chance to cool off.

Making a deliberate effort to identify the emotion can improve your and your child's overall and mental health. An overflow of emotions can often have a physical manifestation in the body—for example, a child experiencing stress or anxiety will often complain of stomach aches—and by managing them better, these physical symptoms will also improve.

### Co-Regulation With Your Child

When your child struggles to manage their own emotions, and especially when you are also experiencing similar emotions, it can be helpful if you do an exercise with your child to calm both of you down. This will help your child realize that they are not alone in experiencing certain negative emotions. You can tell your child something like, "I see you are feeling very sad right now. I'm also feeling sad. Let's help each other feel happy again." This way, you have identified the negative emotions you are both experiencing and the positive emotions you want to have.

Sit with them. If you want, you can put your arm on their shoulder or rub their backs lightly while you do one of these exercises, such as *hot chocolate breathing* or whatever you choose with them. Their close physical proximity to you can also help them overcome their sadness. Once you have both calmed down, look for ways you can bring happiness into the room. Never underestimate the value of laughter, so if you need to, google silly videos.

### *Cry It Out*

If your child's emotions are so extreme that the exercises mentioned above won't help, you may want to allow them to ride it out. Let them sit in a safe space—for example, on their beds—and sit next to them at a distance your child would be comfortable with. Let them experience the emotion by shouting, crying, or punching a pillow if they have to. Gradually, move closer in a subtle way without them necessarily noticing it, until you are sitting next to them. Gently start some physical contact by putting your hand on their shoulder or leg.

Once they have completely calmed down, discuss what happened to them. Name the emotion they were experiencing. Identify what triggered this emotion. Allow them to talk while you listen without interrupting them. Then, explain why their behavior wasn't appropriate in as many details and with as many reasons as you feel are necessary. Be mindful that your child doesn't feel judged for their behavior. Help your child come up with solutions as to how they should react to these emotions in the future. You may have to do this a few times before they learn to change their behavior, but this softer approach can bring great benefits.

### Create an Emotions Chart

If your child is too young or otherwise unable to verbalize their emotions, it can help to create an emotion chart for them. This is something that you can easily do at home or with a basic printer. Create a calendar for every day of the month, then either cut out or print out pictures portraying different emotions. Emojis can work fantastically for this.

Make it a ritual in your home that every night, your child chooses the picture portraying the emotion they experienced on that day and pastes it onto their calendar. This can be very helpful in determining the cause of your child's emotional outbursts and identifying a possible pattern.

Alternatively, if you don't want to do a calendar, you can let them crumple up their pictures of emotions and throw them in the trash. This way they can realize and show their power over the emotion and choose to be "done" with it.

## *Journalling*

If you have an older child struggling with the regulation of their emotions, you may want to encourage them to create an emotions journal. Much like the emotions chart, let your child write in this journal daily about the emotions they experienced and what caused them to feel that way.

Once they get into the habit of doing this, you can encourage them to also make note of how they reacted to the specific emotions, whether they believe this reaction was appropriate, and if not, how they would like to behave going forward. This can help them not only identify their emotions and their emotional triggers but also help them regulate their behavior and emotional responses going forward.

## OTHER EXERCISES TO GET STARTED

If none of these exercises jump out as something that would work for your child, or if you want to incorporate more, I've included some extra exercises that have been proven to help a child struggling with ADHD be more mindful.

## *Mindful Coloring*

Your child might not enjoy coloring due to the constraints of having to color between the lines. In mindful coloring, they don't have to stay in the lines. The purpose of this isn't to create the most beautiful picture that will win awards, but to focus on the sensation of holding a crayon (or whatever other tool they choose to color with) in their hands and the sound it makes as it moves on the paper. This can also help them let go of the idea that if a picture isn't perfectly colored, it's not good enough.

If they don't want to color, you can also let them doodle or draw. Simply creating repeated shapes on a sheet of paper can be very soothing.

## *Create a Maze*

Walking in a maze can help your child become more mindful of the way their body moves and the different muscles used for coordination. This exercise is more effective with younger children. If you have the space, you can use sticks or sidewalk chalk to draw a maze for your child to walk in a tightrope style. If you don't have the space outside, you can create the same effect by using masking tape inside on tile or carpet floors.

When your child does this, make sure they are using slow, calculated movements by putting their entire foot down on the floor with every step they take. If your child seems to be rushing through the steps carelessly, play with their imagination by pretending there is lava all around them.

## *Breath Button*

This is another breathing technique that can be very effective in calming your child down. The idea behind this exercise is to identify at least one object in or around your home and rename it as their *Breath Button*. Whenever your child touches it, they need to pause and take a few deep, mindful breaths.

A good example of something that can be a *Breath Button*, is the doorknob. Every time your child enters or leaves the house or their room, they need to touch this knob. Therefore, they would calm themselves down to focus either on their schoolwork as they leave the home, or the homework when they come back home.

You can also create small *Breath Buttons* that they can keep in their school bag should they struggle with anxiety while in the classroom. They can then seek out this calming technique wherever they go.

## *Playing Games*

There are many games that can help your child become more mindful and aware without even realizing they are busy with a mindful exercise. One of these is the age-old favorite, "I Spy." You can, however, tweak this according to your child's needs. Instead of looking for something starting with a specific letter, you can let them look for things in specific colors, textures, or shapes.

You can also do this to improve their emotional awareness. If you are in a busy place where there are many other people, you can ask them to identify people with specific emotions; for example, "I spy with my little eye someone who is sad." Let them describe the person they are suspecting is showing this emotion in as much detail as they can; for example, "It is the lady sitting five tables from us with the pink hairband and black jacket."

Teach your child to use their "inside voice" by whispering what they see. This will help to teach them to control their body and to be respectful of others' feelings; for example, "Remember to use your inside voice, as it won't be nice for people to think we are talking about them."

### *Yoga*

This is a fantastic exercise to help them become more aware of their body as well as their breathing. There are various videos available online to teach your child how to do different yoga poses. As they are stretching their muscles by doing these poses, let them concentrate on how their muscles feel when they stretch and how their breathing changes. You can do these exercises with your child and turn them into a fun family activity.

### Knitting or Other Finger Exercises

Finger exercises and things like knitting or crocheting are fantastic activities for children with ADHD to get involved in. They require some degree of concentration, coordination, control, and even a little math at times, although it can be extremely calming to do: The repetition involved gives them a sense of control, while the feeling of the yarn on their fingers can be soothing.

Making something with just a string of yarn can also give them a sense of empowerment and accomplishment that they can be proud of. This will help them realize what great things they are capable of achieving and creating, and that they are so much more than their symptoms of ADHD.

### Gardening

Working in the garden can give your child the same benefits as doing finger exercises, such as knitting or crocheting. While knitting is great at developing a child's fine motor skills, digging in a garden improves their gross motor skills. It will also give them a release of their built-up energy.

Give them ownership of a piece of your garden, or give them a pot with some soil in it if you don't have the garden space. Allow them to plant whatever they want, be it flowers, succulents, or vegetables. As they are digging in the garden or planting, let them focus on how the soil or plants feel, and let them take in the smell of the soil, particularly after it has rained or been watered. Let them take care of it by weeding and watering the garden regularly. Don't ever get involved. Even if you see the garden dying because it needs water, remind them to water it. This will teach them what a big impact their care for something can have.

If you fear that the effect of a dying garden will be too much for them, encourage them to opt for hardier plants, such as succulents.

## *Radical Acceptance*

This practice is about accepting things you have no control over, something that is very important for children with ADHD to do. They will likely have many different symptoms of ADHD that they struggle with or are even unable to control. Also, apart from their symptoms, there are always things happening in life that a person has no control over, and harping on them will only bring grief and agony. But accepting that this is part of life can bring you the peace you need; acceptance gives your mind permission to let go of certain things. This will, in turn, help to reduce the anxiety that these uncontrollable events or symptoms may cause your child.

Teach your child that this is a part of life by creating a family ritual; for example, every night as you sit down to eat dinner, let every family member name one thing that happened to them that day that wasn't within their control and that they will have to accept. In the beginning, your child may seem hesitant and feel like it involves too much thinking, but the more you do this, the easier it will become.

By hearing what your child deems uncontrollable, you can get a better insight into what is bothering them. If you can come up with solutions as to how they can better manage these "uncontrollable" events or symptoms, you can help guide them. Otherwise, you can help them accept these things by letting them name their struggles and find the peace they need.

This technique also ties in with distress tolerance, as your child can use acceptance to deal with certain conflicts or stressful situations in their life. By accepting these difficult situations as they are, they will have the peace to look at the best way in which they can react to them.

### *Ride the Wave*

Sometimes the best way for your child to deal with difficult emotions is to ride the wave without reacting to it. This will teach your child that if you have a difficult emotion, such as anger, it will eventually pass, whether you take any action or not.

A helpful way to do this is to let them visualize the waves in the ocean. Let them see their emotion as the wave, and that just like the wave will get smaller and smaller until it eventually dissipates. Nothing anyone does will change the strength of the wave until the wave reaches its natural end. Ultimately, the wave will return to the beach. Similarly, their emotions will return to a place of safety. They don't have to allow this emotion (or wave) to cause them to react in a way that can seem self-destructive.

If your child struggles with visualizing this, you can print out a picture or even get a poster of a wave and put it up in their rooms. There are also various ocean sound clips online that they can play as they look at the picture of the wave, or even an online video of a wave breaking. As they get into the habit of seeing their emotions as waves, they will be able to visualize this much easier.

### Create a Pause Word

Learning how to literally pause their body, thoughts, and emotions can be a very helpful trick to help your child become more mindful. This will help them to manage their stress and anxieties in a healthier way, without reacting in a harsh or negative manner.

Many psychologists believe in creating a "pause" word or phrase that anyone in the family can use when they need to take a breather or when they feel like a fight is about to erupt. This can be something like "code red," "hold," or even just a plain "pause." Whenever someone says this word or phrase, everyone will know that this person is reaching a breaking point and needs to cool off. Everyone will then agree to stop the argument immediately and only resume the argument or conversation once everyone feels calm and ready.

This can be particularly helpful for children with ADHD, whose behavior can seem explosive at times. In the next chapter, we will discuss this in more detail, as well as give more tips on how to deal with explosive behavior in particular.

# 7

# PREVENT AND MANAGE EXPLOSIVE BEHAVIOR

The behavior of children with ADHD can often seem extremely explosive. This can be due to their symptoms resulting in them behaving in a way that seems unacceptable to others or because other people—often their parents—don't know how to cope with their child's behavior and make one parenting mistake after the other.

If you implement the various mindful parenting techniques we've already discussed in the book, you should already be a step ahead of many other parents struggling with the same situation. Luckily, there are many more practical steps you can take daily to prevent and manage your child's explosive behavior.

We will start by discussing some of the reasons why your child's behavior may seem over the top. Then, we will look at what you can do to help your child, including how to remain calm, encourage self-compassion, reward calm behavior, and help your child if they are struggling academically.

## ADHD AND EXPLOSIVE BEHAVIOR

All children will, at some point in their lives, try to push the boundaries. Children with ADHD can often seem a lot more defiant than their neurotypical peers. They may portray a pattern of anger and sometimes even violent behavior, particularly toward authority figures—most often their primary caregivers—in their lives. As we have discussed in Chapter 3, almost half the children (and especially boys) with ADHD will also suffer from ODD.

It can be difficult to determine when your little one is simply being a child with ADHD or whether they may have ODD and need additional professional help to deal with their defiance. Unfortunately, there is no clear line between what is generally considered to be typical childhood defiance and what can be regarded as another mental illness such as ODD. This is often why children who also have ODD are not diagnosed, and as a result, may not receive the treatment they need.

This can result in a break in the relationship between the child and their caregiver or parent, as the parent may not want to do fun activities any more out of fear that the child will react in an explosive manner. However, it is important to remember that the more you withdraw from your child, the more defiant they may become. If you are scared of how your child may behave in public, make an effort to spend time with them at home. Practice the exercises and tips provided here, and chances are you will see an improvement in your child's behavior. It may take time and a lot of patience, but the rewards will be worth it.

Remember that, in most cases, your child isn't acting out of malice. They are purely reacting to their symptoms and the difficulties they are experiencing daily. Some of these can include

- being scared or angry.
- not knowing how else to express their frustrations.
- physical needs, such as hunger or fatigue, that aren't met.
- previous times when you may have given in to their tantrums.
- hyperactivity that makes it very difficult for your child to sit still.
- boredom that children with ADHD find more difficult to tolerate.
- acting on impulses.
- being made to feel ashamed for how they react.

- struggling to concentrate or understand their work at the same pace their neurotypical peers may.
- side effects from the medication they are taking.

Many of these causes of explosive behavior can be successfully reduced by practicing exercises such as radical acceptance and riding the wave. Stay strong and always try to help your child, no matter how dire the situation may seem.

## HELPING YOUR CHILD PREVENT EXPLOSIVE BEHAVIOR

There are many ways in which you can help prevent the explosive behavior that you may have become used to. Always keep in mind that, especially if you've allowed specific types of behavior for a while, you may struggle a bit longer to eliminate or reduce it. But it is possible. Let's look at some of the things you can do to try to improve your child's behavior.

### Don't Label Your Child

When you receive your child's diagnosis, always keep in mind that ADHD doesn't define your child. It is, therefore, important to never label your child or their behavior as being "so ADHD." This can result in your child believing that no matter what they do or how hard they try, they will never be able to overcome their struggles with their symptoms. This can result in even more explosive behavior from your child.

Instead of telling them to "stop being so ADHD," you can say something like, "I can see you are struggling today with some impulsivity. Let's see if we can do something to make it easier for you." This will help them realize that they are not only understood, but that you care for them and want to help them through their difficulties.

### Give Them the Tools

A child with ADHD often struggles with a lack of logic, reasoning, and memory, which can reduce their tolerance for dealing with situations that cause them frustration. Help them overcome this by explaining events that they may not understand and helping them by reasoning through their struggles. Listen carefully to what aspects of the problem they don't understand and guide them instead of instructing them to find the best solution or outcome.

Also, make sure the expectations you set for them are realistic and within their skill set. Your child may not receive the grades you want them to. Keep the limitations that the symptoms of ADHD can cause in mind and try to avoid putting unnecessary stress on them. This can easily result in explosive behavior that could've been avoided. Always help your child understand that as long as they try their best and work as hard as they can, you are satisfied with their achievements.

## *Nobody Is Perfect*

Adding to the importance of being realistic in your expectations of them, it is important to remember that nobody's perfect. In the same way that you will make mistakes as a parent, your child will also make choices that you will likely not agree with. Reacting negatively to their mistakes will only cause them more frustration and increase the likelihood of emotional and explosive outbursts. Accept that your child will make mistakes, and help them through this by discussing where their choices may have been wrong and what they can learn from the experience.

## *Don't Get Trapped by Anger*

Being angry won't help you solve the problems you may experience with your child, and will definitely not help you improve your child's behavior or your relationship with them. Try your best to avoid hanging on to anger or reacting to it. Use the techniques listed in the previous chapters to calm down before you discuss the situation with your child, as this can help to avoid heated arguments. It is natural that there will be times when you disagree with your child. The easiest way you will resolve this is by accepting this fact.

### *Prioritize Your Child's Problems*

Once you start to carefully look at the problems your child may have and that you would like to address, it is important that you don't try to take on all their problems at the same time. It can be helpful to prioritize their problems. If their behavior is causing safety issues, they should be addressed first. Take on the most urgent problems first, and work on no more than three at a time. Then, gradually add more problems as your child is able to improve their behavior with little to no effort.

## REMAINING CALM IN THE FACE OF EXPLOSIVE BEHAVIOR

Apart from the various calming techniques we have already discussed, there's more you as a parent can do to try to remain calm no matter how explosive your child's behavior may be. Let's look at some exercises you can do to become a calmer parent in the midst of the chaos that your life may currently be in.

### *Practice Self-Care*

You need to take care of yourself before you can take care of others. Think of the oxygen masks on an airplane. You are always advised to put a mask on yourself before you attempt to assist others. The same is true about self-care. If you don't take care of yourself, you will be depleting yourself physically, mentally, and emotionally and, as a result, won't be able to help your child.

Make sure you are getting enough restful sleep, eating healthy meals, exercising, and making time for yourself to spend selfishly doing something you really enjoy. During this time, ask your partner to take over the parenting duties or arrange a playdate for your child or a babysitter so you can focus only on yourself without feeling guilty or worrying about what your child may get up to while you are taking care of yourself.

### *Want the Change*

Changing the explosive behavior that has become the norm in your home can take a lot of work and effort. To make this slightly easier, always remind yourself of why you are doing this and how badly you want to bring change to your and your child's lives. It can be very helpful to create a mantra for yourself that you can repeat during these challenging times, such as "I will not scream," "I love my child," "I want things to change," or "I can remain calm."

### Choose Your Time

As much as you should try your best to avoid interacting with your child when you are overly annoyed or furious with them, you should also consider your child's feelings. If your little one is having a tough time or feels very tired, you may want to give them some space and wait for a better time before you address your issues with them. Just because it is always best to discuss difficulties as soon as possible, it doesn't have to mean that you should do it right away. You can do it later by referring back to the event by saying something like, "I want to talk about something that happened earlier today."

### Respect Your child

In the same way you want your child to respect you, you should always respect your child. They have the right to their own thoughts, feelings, and privacy. As long as they aren't in physical danger or too young to understand the consequences of their actions, you can give them some privacy when they need it.

### Reward Calm Behavior

If you've implemented rules and plans for how meltdowns should be handled, it can be helpful to reward your child when they behave according to these rules. This can be anything from points on a chart where they can earn a bigger reward to extra screen time. By rewarding calm behavior instead of reacting to the negative behavior, you put emphasis on the good instead of the bad and teach your child to try to correct their behavior by themselves.

### *Discuss Instead of Dictate*

Your child may be more motivated to correct their behavior if they played a role in setting the rules. It is therefore important to discuss these rules with them instead of dictating to them how they should behave.

Listen to them when they talk to you. Ask them how they believe the problem could be solved and consider their suggestions. This doesn't mean you should always give in to their demands, but instead, come to a compromise you may both be comfortable with.

Let's look at an example of this. Say your child has a set bedtime of 8:00 p.m. daily, but one night they are still playing a game when it's time to go to bed. They beg you for only 10 more minutes to finish the game. You now have a choice: Either allow the 10 minutes and let them go to bed peacefully, or potentially deal with a meltdown that may last an hour, if not more. You may want to allow the extra 10 minutes just to keep the peace, but you may worry that this will create a habit of your child continuously trying to push their bedtime.

You can then say, "I will allow this tonight only, but tomorrow we will need to have a discussion about your bedtime and how you can use your time more effectively so that you can finish your game and get to bed in time. If you don't get a good night's sleep, you may be too tired at school the next day and struggle to concentrate even more."

Follow through with this by having a discussion with them. See what you can cut out of their schedule to make more time for the game that is important to your child. Remember, just as it is important for you to practice self-care, so is it for your child to relax and do something they enjoy.

Again, always remember that you shouldn't have to compromise every time your child whines about something. You are still their parent and should implement rules. However, for the sake of maintaining calm and helping your child feel like they are in charge of certain aspects of their life, you may want to consider making some compromises in a controlled environment.

If your child continues to push their luck on aspects that you aren't willing to budge on, warn them that this type of behavior will result in them losing the privilege of changing their schedule, and follow through with this threat should it continue.

## *Stay Committed*

When you raise a child with a neurodiversity such as ADHD, it is important that you stay committed to helping your child bring about the change they may need. Never give up on your child, no matter how difficult things may seem. Show your children the unconditional love they deserve.

## ENCOURAGING SELF-COMPASSION

Helping your child—and yourself—to be more compassionate can lay the groundwork for positive changes. Increasing their self-compassion can bring about changes and help them thrive in a way that neither you nor they may have ever thought possible.

To help your child with this, you can do an exercise that can not only bring about more mindfulness, but also help this positive attitude become more ingrained. To do this exercise, discuss a time limit with your child. This can be anything from 5 to 15 minutes. Once you've determined the limit, set a timer and start the exercise:

- Let them sit or lie in a comfortable position in a quiet space where they can be calm and focus only on what they are feeling.

- Encourage them to close their eyes, or stare at a specific object that won't be distracting.
- Ask your child to take a few deep breaths. Help them to clear their minds and rid themselves of any worrying thoughts or self-recrimination. Let them focus only on their breathing and how their bodies move with each breath.
- Once their breathing settles, let them experience and accept their thoughts. Encourage them to express their thoughts out loud so that you can not only know what they are thinking, but be in a position where you can help them deal with them more effectively.
- Help them to calm down by saying things like, "Everyone feels like this at times," or "I've also felt like that but it doesn't have to be like this forever."
- After they've accepted this, ask them to repeat a confirmation phrase with you, such as, "I can find strength within myself," "I can get over this," "This won't continue forever," or "If I'm kind to myself, I can accomplish everything."
- If your child gets distracted, calmly bring their focus back to the topic you are discussing with them or the phrase they should be repeating.
- Let them continue with this phrase and breathing until the timer goes off.

The more compassionate they are toward themselves, the easier it will be for them to deal with their difficult situations and overcome the challenges they may experience.

## HELP YOUR CHILD MANAGE ACADEMIC EXPECTATIONS

A major cause of frustration for many children with ADHD is concentrating and focusing on their schoolwork so that they can achieve academically. It's always important to remember that if your child isn't achieving the academic results you or the school may expect from them, it doesn't mean they don't have the intelligence to achieve greatness; the consequences of the symptoms of their ADHD have nothing to do with their intelligence. They may just need some extra help.

Due to their inability to pay attention, they may miss some of the teachings in class and take a bit longer to understand new concepts. However, once they have the lightbulb moment, they are able to achieve academically. Let's look at specific ways in which you can assist your child with their schoolwork.

### *Be Consistent With Your Rules*

Even though their impulses can make it difficult to follow rules, this can make a big difference in your child's ability to perform. We've already mentioned the importance of following a strict routine, and this is even more so when it comes to schoolwork. It can be helpful to create a study schedule for your child. This way they will know exactly when they need to study and how long it will be before they have their next break. Otherwise, they may spend more time focusing on how long they still need to work than on the actual work.

Apart from creating a study schedule, you may want to consider getting them an analog clock to put on their desk so that they can keep track of time. This type of clock is particularly effective, as they will be able to visualize exactly how far the timer must go before they can take their break. Also, the ticking sound that the second's arm on the clock will create can be soothing to your child.

Always keep in mind that it can be difficult for your child to shift gears when moving from one subject to the next. They are often unable to make the transition from math to biology like many neurotypical children can. If this is the case for your child, schedule a break in between the different subjects. Let them pack away all their books on the subject they have finished working on to physically make the shift and avoid distractions.

### *Reduce Distractions*

Children with ADHD are often easily distracted, so it is important to let them work in a space where there is as little outside stimulation as possible. Even a window can be a problem, as your child may be more interested in what's happening outside than in their work. If possible, let them sit with their backs to the window in a space where there is either no television or where all electronics are switched off.

Also, look at what clutter there may be on the surface they work on. Let them only keep the stationery, such as a single pen, pencil, and eraser, on the desk, and only the books they are currently working on. When it comes to stationery, keep it as simple as possible. Decorative pens with animal figurines on them may look cute, but they will only serve to distract your child even more.

It can also be helpful to play white noise in the background, as this can be a soothing sound for children with ADHD and help them to concentrate. If you find your child is constantly singing or humming while they are working, leave them to do this. While you might think this singing is distracting them from their work, it actually serves the opposite purpose, as it helps them to concentrate.

### Give Proper Feedback

All children benefit from receiving frequent and proper feedback. Children with ADHD often make small mistakes in their work, such as confusing math symbols like plus and minus. If you give them continuous feedback while they are working, you can help them correct their work immediately, which can drastically improve their self-confidence.

Keep negative feedback as short as you can by explaining what they did wrong, why it was wrong, and helping them figure out what the correct action should've been. Praise them for what they did right, no matter how small and insignificant it may seem. Focus on the positives as much as you can.

A helpful way to deal with giving feedback is by sandwiching the negative comments in between the positive ones. For example, start the feedback session by commenting on things they did right and how proud you are of this. Then, explain what they did wrong. Follow up on this negative feedback by focusing on something else they did right. This way, they will still learn from their mistakes, but they will feel much better about themselves.

### Give Frequent Breaks

All children need breaks in between their work, as they are only capable of concentrating for a specific amount of time depending on their age group. This is even more true for children with ADHD. Not only is their attention span shorter than that of neurotypical children, but they will also struggle to sit still for long periods of time.

When they have these breaks, allow them to move around to get rid of some of their energy. Let them have something to drink—preferably a glass of water, as you don't want to add to their energy levels by letting them consume sugary drinks—and a healthy snack. Give them a five-minute warning before their break is over so that they can mentally start to prepare themselves for going back to work.

### Don't Overload Your Child

Try not to overload your child with too much work. Even though they will be required to complete the same amount of work as their neurotypical peers, help to make this easier for them by breaking their workload up into doable chunks.

Also, plan your child's schedule according to their optimal times for concentration. Many psychologists believe that in the three to six hours after waking in the morning, a person's ability to perform will be at its highest. This may be different for your child, so it can be well worth your time to pay attention to when they perform at their best. Schedule their most difficult or most important tasks for the times when they are most alert.

Let them start their day by doing an easy task that they can complete without using much concentration. This can help give them the confidence they need to tackle the more difficult tasks. Alternatively, let them start with the task they dislike the most. Knowing that they've completed this disliked task can also boost their self-esteem, as they know the worst is done and can look forward to tasks they enjoy more. Play around with the order of your child's tasks until you've discovered the correct order that works best for your youngster.

### Give Support

Your child may need extra help understanding their schoolwork. Try to stay as patient as you can, even if you have to explain the same concept five different ways to try to get them to understand it. Remember, their brains are wired differently, and their memory may be affected by this.

Apart from explaining the work to them, there are many different ways in which you can try to give your child the extra support they may need. This can include doing extra classes or in the form of peer support. Having a "study buddy" may help your child remember things more easily and can even increase their focus. If you opt for this, just make sure you keep a close eye on them. As much as this study buddy may help your child, they may also serve as a distraction. If you find that this is the case, stop immediately and look for other ways to benefit your child.

# 8

# IMPROVE SELF-CONTROL IN YOUR CHILD

Having appropriate self-control is a very important life skill that all people should have. This helps you successfully integrate with others in a social and, eventually, professional environment. Most children learn the necessary skills for self-control as they grow up. However, this can be a more difficult task for children with ADHD, particularly those struggling to control their impulses.

You can help your child learn this skill through various easy exercises to improve their executive function, delay gratification, use of visual prompts, and teach self-control. In this final chapter, I will give you various proven tips and strategies on how you can successfully help your child with this. But first, let's take a deeper look at why children with ADHD may struggle with self-control.

## ADHD AND SELF-CONTROL

Children with ADHD often struggle to control their impulses and, as a result, fail to see the potential consequences of their actions until it's too late. This can result in sometimes severe difficulty with self-control, as they are, in many instances, physically and mentally unable to hit the brakes to think about their actions.

The struggles that these children may have at school, in social situations, and with regulating their emotions can cause a lot of frustration, stress, and anxiety in them. Unfortunately, these children are often stuck in a vicious cycle; the more they struggle with self-control and resisting their impulses, the more they may become frustrated with themselves, and the more their frustration levels increase, the weaker their self-control can become.

What can make self-control an even more difficult skill to learn is that children with ADHD often don't understand specific social rules or don't realize that they are breaking them until it is too late. They may struggle to read the social cues of other people, and in their habit of interrupting others and conversations, their lack of self-control can become a big cause of frustration for the people in their lives.

## IMPROVING YOUR CHILD'S EXECUTIVE FUNCTION CAPACITY

One way of helping your child develop better self-control is to improve their executive function. This is a person's ability to follow instructions, pay attention, plan, and handle more than one task at the same time. It can provide a filter for the brain to avoid distractions, limit impulses, prioritize, and achieve goals. This filter uses three functions of the brain: Memory, mental flexibility, and self-control.

These three functions are things that people with ADHD often struggle with. No person is born with these skills. They are taught and developed over time. However, children with neurodiversity, such as ADHD, may need more help to acquire these skills. Let's look at how you can help your child with this.

### *Card and Board Games*

These types of games provide many more benefits than simply having fun together as a family. It can also improve a child's memory, concentration, cognitive flexibility, and self-control. These types of games will force your child to focus and adjust according to what the game dictates, not their own wishes. Games that require the players to act quickly due to strict time limits can be fantastic at improving attention, as the child will know they will lose the game if they don't focus completely on what they are doing. Games that require your child to come up with strategies or plan a few moves ahead will teach your child about planning and, as a result, improve your child's cognitive ability and memory.

## *Physical Activities*

There are many physical activities that you can do with your child that can help to improve their executive function. Games such as *Musical Statues, Duck, Duck, Goose, Red Light, Green Light*, or *What Time Is It, Mr. Fox?* can be fantastic in helping your child develop their memory, ability to resist their urges, and memory. By doing these types of activities with your child, you also help them get rid of some of their built-up energy and you will get to laugh together. As I've said before, never underestimate the impact that laughter can have on your and your child's mental health, executive function, and your relationship with your child.

## *Movement Games*

There is a reason why a game such as *Charades* has remained so popular and is so frequently recommended by child psychologists and occupational therapists. This type of game is great for practicing your child's memory, letting them push their inhibitions to a healthy level, reducing their impulsivity, and being creative. In younger children, songs that provide auditory challenges can bring the same benefits. Examples of these types of songs include *Boom Chicka Boom* and *ChaCha Slide*. Do these movements with your little one, have fun together, and see how your child's executive function is improving while they are having a good time.

### Quiet Activities

As much as it can be very beneficial for your child to develop by using games and songs, you should never disregard the importance of quiet activities. Depending on your child's age, these activities can include building puzzles, doing word searches, completing crossword puzzles, and doing Sudoku, to name only a few. These games will require them to resist their impulses, sit still for long enough to complete a task, concentrate, and solve problems, which requires using their memory and cognitive flexibility.

If your child struggles with completing these types of activities, you can help them with them. Just make sure that you don't take over and complete the task for them. Find the balance between allowing them to struggle so that they can develop these functions and letting their frustration levels reach a point where they may have a meltdown or refuse to do these activities again. Help them to understand the importance of these activities and the value they can bring to their lives without pushing them beyond their own limits.

## TEACHING DELAYED GRATIFICATION

Many children with ADHD will seek out activities that will give them instant gratification. Even if they know a bigger reward may be waiting for them if they're able to wait, they would struggle to do this and, eventually, give in to their urges by accepting the smaller reward instead of waiting.

Think of this as the well-known test on giving a child one sweet. They can have this sweet at any time, but they won't get more. However, if they are willing to wait for 10 minutes, they would get five sweets instead of just one. Young children and children with ADHD will struggle to wait the full 10 minutes and will likely eat the one sweet sometime between five and eight minutes. If your child had better self-control, they would be able to wait a few more minutes and get the extra four sweets.

This example can be applied to many different aspects of your child's life. Let's look at their schoolwork, for example. If they aren't focusing and concentrating, they may only get a 15-minute break. But, if they apply their focus and work faster, they may be able to take a 30-minute break. There are many different ways in which you can help to improve their ability to work toward a bigger reward or delayed gratification.

### Reward Self-Control

When you give your child a task where they need to use self-control, it is important that you recognize the efforts your child is making in trying to wait. For example, you may tell your child that you need them to clean their room, unpack the dishwasher, and put their laundry in the hamper. Put a piece of cake on the kitchen counter or at a place where they will have to walk past often to test their self-control in not touching the cake.

If they are able to complete all these tasks, they can have that piece. If they can't complete their tasks, they can't get the cake. If they take a bit before completing their tasks, have another form of punishment ready, such as reducing screen time or not taking them to see the movie they've been wanting to see for a while.

Give them a time limit to complete the task and set the timer so that they will know exactly how much time they have left. Praise them for the progress they are making, and if your child is able to complete their tasks on time and have their cake, reward them with another surprise; for example, increase their screen time.

### Use Their Distractions

If your child is struggling with self-control and waiting for their reward, let them use a distraction to make the time pass more quickly. This can distract them from the sweet in front of them and help them wait for the five sweets they will get in 10 minutes. Some distraction tools you can recommend your child try out include

- counting forward and backward.
- drawing a picture or color in.
- doing a household chore.
- focusing on something else, such as reading.
- getting the body moving by doing exercises or yoga.
- practicing mindfulness through meditation.

### Make "If-Then" Plans

Encourage them to make "if-then" plans, as this will help your child to not only deal with disappointments easier but also improve their ability to wait for a reward. For example, your child may want to earn extra pocket money. They can plan this: If the weather is nice tomorrow, then I will wash the car and get money. Should it be rainy weather the next day, your child will then know that they will have to wait a bit longer for their reward.

## *Positive Self-Talk*

Positive self-talk and affirmations can make a big difference in your child's ability to succeed and wait for a bigger reward. However, many people don't realize the big impact that this can have. A quick exercise can help your child understand the power that this can bring:

- Ask your child to hold their arm out straight. Tell them to resist you as you try to push their arm down to the side. Most children will be able to focus on this to make sure their arm stays up.
- Now, let him repeat a negative phrase 10 times, and make sure to count with your fingers on your free hand so they can track how many times they've said it. An example of a phrase can be, "I'm weak and worthless."
- Once they've repeated this phrase, push at their arm again. You may find that you can now push their arm down easily. Explain to them that the only difference between the first and second time you pushed at their arm, was the negative self-talk.
- Flip this around by letting them repeat a phrase again. This time, let them say a positive affirmation, such as, "I'm strong and worthy." Again, count on your fingers to make sure you're repeating the phrase 10 times.

- Now, try to push on their arm again. You will likely find that you may struggle to push their arm down. Some children may even feel so empowered that you won't be able to move their arms at all. Again, remind them that the only difference again was the positive affirmations they've been repeating.

Ask them how they felt after both instances, first with the negative phrase and then after the positive affirmation. Explain to them that they can have that amazing, empowered feeling by repeating a positive phrase every time they experience difficulties in their life. Some self-talk affirmations that you can teach your child include:

- I am worthy.
- I am strong.
- I am capable.
- I can be successful.
- I can achieve greatness.
- I can finish my work.
- I can concentrate.

If you want, you can print some of these out and paste them on the walls of your child's room. You can even make small cards with affirmations on them that they can put in their school bags to refer to during the day when they're feeling down.

## TEACHING SELF-CONTROL

While the exercises given above will help your child to wait for their rewards, there are many other ways you can help your child increase their self-control. Always remember that due to your child's ADHD, they are often unable to self-regulate. Helping them control their urges and modify their behavior can make a big difference in their lives.

### *Discipline Appropriately*

A big part of teaching self-control has to do with their ability to understand the consequences of their actions. To do this, it is important to work on the way you discipline your child. Let's look at how you can do this.

- **Choose the right punishment**: Always make sure that the punishment fits the crime. If your child is acting on their impulses, they shouldn't be punished by losing all their privileges. An appropriate punishment for misbehaving at the dinner table may be to dismiss them from the table without dessert. If they hurt their sibling, a harsher punishment may be appropriate.

- **Let minor things slide**: There may be times when accidents happen and your child misbehaves in a minor way. Your child may spill juice when they pour themself a glass. Talk to them about this and explain that if they slow down and take more care when they do things like this, they will make fewer messes. Pick your battles and remember that if it has been a minor misstep, you may want to simply give a warning without punishment.

- **Let your child be accountable**: When your child misbehaves, it's important to make sure they understand why their actions have been wrong. Make sure the punishment is immediate, as your child may struggle to understand the consequences of their actions and the reasons for the punishment when there is delayed punishment. Let them be accountable for their actions.

## *Prepare for Impulses*

No matter how much you try, there will likely be instances where your child will act on their impulses. If you keep this in mind and prepare for these reactions, you may be able to handle this better and stay calm. Have structures and routines in place, and if they do act on their impulses, be ready to stop this behavior immediately by explaining to them why their actions are inappropriate and guiding them to realize how they should rather behave.

You may also want to introduce a specific phrase for when your child feels their impulses are getting the better of them; for example, "urge coming." When this happens, praise your child for giving the warning and help them to calm down so that they can manage these urges more effectively.

### Create Behavior Cards

Some children with ADHD may benefit from having physical reminders of how they should behave. Since you aren't always with them, it can be helpful to make behavior cards for them that they can take with them to school to remind them of the agreed-upon rules for their behaviors. These can include things such as "counting to 10 before you talk" so that they can consider whether what they're saying is appropriate, "raising your hand before you speak," and "sitting still while you need to work."

### How Long Can You Sit Still?

You can help your child to gain more self-control by doing simple challenges with them. An example of this is seeing how long your child can sit still. Time them as they sit and write down the time. Do the challenge again later or the next day and time them again. Let them see if they can beat their previous time. Track their improvement and praise them as much as possible.

## USING VISUAL PROMPTS

Since children with ADHD often struggle with inattentiveness and following instructions, they may forget what you've said shortly after you're done speaking. If you find that this is the case for your child, using visual prompts can make a huge difference. For example, if your child struggles with finishing their homework, you may want to put up a poster asking them something like, "Is your homework done?" Only once they have finished their homework are they allowed to take the poster down. Similar posters or visual prompts can be created for other chores, such as "Put your laundry in the hamper," "Clean your room," or "Pack away your toys."

If making posters won't work for you or your child, you can also create checklists for them, where they can literally tick off tasks as they've been completed. You may also want to consider putting a whiteboard in their room so they can create their own checklist. Go over the checklists with your child daily to make sure all the tasks have been completed and help them come up with tasks to include on their checklist for the next day.

# CONCLUSION

You now have all the skills you need to help your child manage the symptoms of their ADHD more successfully, become more mindful, manage their emotions better, and increase their self-control. You have a better understanding of their ADHD and the potential impact their symptoms can have on their lives, and, as a result, you understand your child a lot better.

You realize what a positive impact being more mindful in your parenting style can have on your child and how important it is to adjust your style to protect and enhance your child's mental wellness. Let's recap some of the techniques we have discussed in the book:

- Dialectical behavioral techniques that consist of four pillars:

- Mindfulness
- Interpersonal effectiveness using the acronyms *THINK*, *FAST*, and *GIVE*.
- Distress tolerance
- Emotional regulation
- Prevent and manage your child's explosive behavior.
- Remain calm in difficult situations.
- Encourage self-compassion.
- Help your child improve their academic performance.
- Work with your child to develop their self-control.

You can be the parent you've always wanted to be. You can have a happy and successful child despite having ADHD. You can remove (or at the very least, reduce) the explosive emotions and behaviors in your home. You now have all the tools and techniques you will need to achieve this. Go out there, use them, and create the life and relationship with your child that you've always desired.

If you enjoyed the book and found the exercises and tips provided to be life-changing for you and your child, please help me to assist others by leaving a review on Amazon.

# REFERENCES

*ADHD Comorbidities: ODD, OCD, Learning Disabilities, Autism, Bipolar.* (n.d.). ADDitude. https://www.additudemag.com/category/adhd-add/related-conditio ns/

*Attention deficit hyperactivity disorder (ADHD) in children.* (2019). John Hopkins Medicine. https://www.hopkinsmedicine.org/health/conditions-and-diseases/adhdadd

Bandari, S. (2022, September 27). *ADHD in children.* WebMD. https://www.webmd.com/add-adhd/childhood-adhd/adhd-children

Barrow, K. (2022, July 13). *Why is my child so angry?!* ADDitude. https://www.additudemag.com/adhd-odd-why-is-my-child-angry/

Bhandari, S. (2021, April 21). *ADHD or Tourette's: What is the difference?* WebMD. https://www.webmd.com/add-adhd/childhood-adhd/adhd-vs-tourettes-syndrome

Bredehoft, D. J. (2020, January 7). *Strategies to teach children delayed gratification.* Psychology Today. https://www.psychologytoday.com/us/blog/the-age-overindulgence/202001/strategies-teach-children-delayed-gratification

Broadbent, E. (2022, January 21). *Does everyone have ADHD? How flippant neurotypical claims hurt.* ADDitude. https://www.additudemag.com/does- everyone-have-adhd/

Chen, C. (n.d.). *Is it ADHD or typical toddler behavior? Ten early signs of ADHD risk in preschool-age children.* Kennedy Krieger Institute. https://www.kennedy krieger.org/stories/Is-it-adhd-or-typical-toddler-behavior-ten-early-signs-adhd-risk-preschool-age-children

Cooney, M. (2022). *The benefits of mindful parenting for ADHD kids.* Study.com. https://study.com/blog/the-benefits-of-mindful-parenting-for-adhd-kids.html

*DBT for attention deficit hyperactivity disorder.* (n.d.). DBT Center of Marin. https://dbtmarin.com/dbt-for-attention-deficit-hyperactivity-disorder

Debros, K., Willard, C., & Buck, E. (n.d.). *Easy mindfulness exercises for kids with ADHD*. https://utahparentcenter.org/wp-content/uploads/2020/04/Easy- Mindfulness-Exercises-for-Kids-with-ADHD.pdf

*Does ADHD raise the risk of mental health issues?* (n.d.). Understood. https://www.understood.org/en/articles/does-adhd-raise-risk-mental-health-issues

*Executive function and self-regulation.* (2015). Center on the Developing Child at Harvard University; Harvard University. https://developingchild.harvard. edu/science/key-concepts/executive-function/

*Five DBT skills to help your kids manage stress.* (2020, July 9). https://www.youthranch.org/blog/5-dbt-skills-to-help-your-kids-manage-stress

Gnanavel, S., Sharma, P., Kaushal, P., & Hussain, S. (2019). *Attention deficit hyperactivity disorder and comorbidity: A review of literature.* World Journal of Clinical Cases, 7(17), 2420–2426. https://doi.org/10.12998/wjcc.v7.i17.2420

*How to handle your ADHD child's explosive behavior.* (2018, March 16). The ADHD Centre. https://www.adhdcentre.co.uk/handle-your-childs-explosive- behaviour/

Herndon, J. (2021, May 3). *Is ADHD considered a mental illness?* Healthline. https://www.healthline.com/health/adhd/is-adhd-a-mental-illness

Higuera, V. (2019, January 30). *ADHD and ODD: What's the connection?* Healthline Media. https://www.healthline.com/health/adhd/adhd-and-odd

*Impulse control strategies for school and home.* (2022, October 28). ADDitude. https://www.additudemag.com/impulse-control-strategies-adhd-students/

*Is ADHD a serious condition?* (2016, September 3). The American Professional Society of ADHD and Related Disorders. https://apsard.org/is-adhd-a-serious-condition/

Kelly, K. (n.d.). *What causes trouble with self-control.* Understood. https://www.understood.org/en/articles/what-causes-trouble-with-self-control

Kinman, T. (2012, December 17). *Gender differences in ADHD Symptoms.* Healthline Media. https://www.healthline.com/health/adhd/adhd-symptoms-in-girls-and- boys

Lockett, E. (2022, March 14). *What are the most common signs of ADHD?* Healthline. https://www.healthline.com/health/adhd/signs#signs-in-women

Lovering, N. (2022, May 18). *ADHD and emotions: Relationship and tips to manage.* Healthline. https://www.healthline.com/health/adhd/emotional-regulation#tips

Low, K. (2018). *8 simple school strategies for students with ADHD.* Verywell Mind. https://www.verywellmind.com/help-for-students-with-adhd-20538

Marcin, A. (2019, August 21). *Mindful parenting: Definition, examples, and benefits.* Healthline. https://www.healthline.com/health/parenting/mindful-parenting

Miller, C. (2017, October 3). *ADHD and behavior problems.* Child Mind Institute. https://childmind.org/article/adhd-behavior-problems/

*Mood disorders & ADHD.* (2015, November 21). Healthy Children. https://www.healthychildren.org/English/health-issues/conditions/adhd/Pages/Mood-Disorders-ADHD.aspx

Mooney, J. (2022, January 16). *Accepting your ADHD diagnosis: Success with attention deficit.* Additude. https://www.additutdemag.com/adhd-myths-accept-diagnosis-success-story/

Morgan, K. K. (2022, May 24). *Childhood ADHD vs. conduct disorder.* WebMD. https://www.webmd.-

com/add-adhd/childhood-adhd/adhd-vs-conduct-disorder

Mörstedt, B., Corbisiero, S., Bitto, H., & Stieglitz, R.-D. (2015). *Attention-deficit hyperactivity disorder (ADHD) in adulthood: Concordance and differences between self and informant perspectives on symptoms and functional impairment.* PLOS ONE, 10(11), e0141342. https://doi.org/10.1371/journal. pone.0141342

Myers, R. (n.d.). *10 concentration and focus building techniques for children with ADHD.* Empowering Parents. https://www.empoweringparents.com/articile/5- simple-concentration-building-techniques-for-kids-with-adhd/

*Oppositional defiant disorder (ODD) - Diagnosis and treatment.* (2018). Mayo Clinic. https://www.mayoclinic.org/diseases-conditions/oppositional-defiant-disorder/diagnosis-treatment/drc-20375837

Perles, K. (2022, March 18). *Dealing with difficult child behavior? 6 ways to keep your cool.* Care. https://www.care.com/c/dealing-with-difficult-child-behavior-6-ways

*Protecting the health of children with ADHD.* (2019b, October 7). Centers for Disease Control and Prevention. https://www.cdc.gov/ncbddd/adhd/features/ protecting-adhd-children.html

Rawe, J. (n.d.). *The ADHD brain.* Understood. https://www.understood.org/ en/articles/adhd-and-the-brain

*Research on ADHD.* (2019a, April 19). Centers for Disease Control and Prevention. https://www.cdc.-gov/ncbddd/adhd/research.html

Saline, S. (2018, August 6). *5 common mistakes parents make with their ADHD kids and how to fix them.* The Philidephia Inquirer. https://www.inquirer.com/ philly/health/kids-families/5-common-mistakes-parents-make-with-their-adhd-kids-and-how-to-fix-them-20180806.html

Schimelpfening, N. (2022, July 22). *What to know about dialectical behavior therapy.* Verywell Mind. https://www.verywellmind.com/dialectical-behavior-therapy

Silver, L. (2022, September 29). *The neuroscience of the ADHD brain.* ADDitude. https://www.additudemag.-com/neuroscience-of-adhd-brain/

Sinfield, J. (2021, January 21). *The relationship between ADHD and learning disabilities.* Verywell Mind. https://www.verywellmind.com/is-adhd-a-learning-disability-4116126

Smith, J. (2021, June 29). *5 lessons I've learned while parenting a child with ADHD*. FastBraiin. https://www.fastbraiin.com/blogs/blog/5-lessons-ive-learned-in-adhd-parenting

Spencer, T., Biederman, J., & Wilens, T. (1999). *Attention deficit hyperactivity disorder and comorbidity*. Pediatric Clinics of North America, 46(5), 915–927. https://doi.org/10.1016/s0031-3955(05)70163-2

Stern, K. (2001). *A treatment study of children with attention deficit hyperactivity disorder*. Office of Justice Programs

Story, C. M. (2017, April 17). *Relationship between ADHD and anxiety*. Healthline Media. https://www.healthline.com/health/adhd-and-anxiety

Sunrisertc. (2017, August 18). *4 steps to happy relationships*. Sunrise Residential Treatment Center. https://sunrisertc.com/interpersonal-effectiveness

Swaim, E. (2022, May 2). *What's the connection between ADHD and self-esteem?* Healthline. https://www.healthline.com/health/adhd/adhd-and-self-esteem

*Talking with your child about ADHD*. (2017, April 27). Children and Adults with Attention Deficit Hyperactivity Disorder. https://Chadd.org/adhd-weekly/ talking-with-your-child-about-adhd/

Tull, M. (2013, July 30). *Distress tolerance in post-traumatic stress disorder*. Verywell Mind. https://www.verywellmind.com/distress-tolerance-2797294

Villines, Z. (2021, July 9). *Tantrums and ADHD: Causes and how to deal with them*. Medical News Today. https://www.medicalnewstoday.com/articles/tantrums-and-adhd

Wait, M. (2015, May 12). *How to recognize ADHD symptoms at every age*. WebMD. https://www.webmd.com/add-adhd/childhood-adhd/adhd-symptoms-age

Watson, S. (2022, March 31). *What is disruptive mood dysregulation disorder?* ADDitude. https://www.additudemag.com/disruptive-mood-dysregulation-disorder-and-adhd/

*What is ADHD?* (2020, April 8). Centers for Disease Control and Prevention. https://www.cdc.gov/ncbddd/adhd/facts.html#:~:text=ADHD%20is%20one%20of%20the

*What it looks like to accept your ADHD*. (n.d.). Take Control ADHD. https://takecontroladhd.com/blog/category/what-it-looks-like-to-accept-your-adhd

Willard, C. (2022, April 22). *Teen stress is very real—and manageable with these exercises*. ADDitude.

https://www.additudemag.com/slideshows/mindfulness-exercises-for-teens-adhd/

Zeigler, C. (2022, September 7). *How teachers can help every student shine.* ADDitude. https://www.additudemag.com/teaching-strategies-for-students-with-adhd/

Made in the USA
Las Vegas, NV
07 November 2023

80412057R00111